LIVING INTO ART

LIVING INTO ART

Journeys Through Collage

LINDSAY WHITING

Paper Lantern®
Illuminating Gifts

Paper Lantern
P.O. Box 1871
Boyes Hot Springs, CA 95416
Ph: 707-935-7001
Fax: 707-935-7750
email: Lindsay@paperlantern.biz
www.paperlantern.biz

ISBN: 978-0-615-18294-0
Printed in China on recycled paper with soy inks

Cover collage by Catherine McIntyre
Book Design by Campana Design
Portrait photos by Don Kellogg Photography

Please note that collages contained in *Living into Art* were created from a wide range of recycled, commercial books, calendars, magazines and collected images for the purpose of personal expression. This book is meant to inspire its readers as well as exemplify certain concepts. It is not intended as a prescriptive work. In no way does this publication serve as a substitute for therapeutic or other forms of professional assistance.

To Barbara and Audrey with gratitude and love

To the collage studio artists: past, present and to come

{ contents }

{ acknowledgements }

I did not choose to write this book—it chose me. It seized my imagination, grabbed me by the hand, and transported me to places that cannot be seen or touched, but moved my heart. I am truly grateful to the many people who showed me the way.

I am most grateful to the Sonoma Collage Studio artists featured here in these chapters. They welcomed me into their lives by generously and candidly sharing themselves, along with their art. I am thankful and humbled by their trust and encouragement, which have allowed me to bring their stories to readers. I also want to acknowledge the audacious vision of Audrey von Hawley and Barbara Jacobsen, the founders of the Sonoma Collage Studio. They never wavered in their consistent support, and showed remarkable flexibility in allowing me to tinker under the hood of their marvelous invention.

I want to thank Inner Ocean Publishing and Hal Zina Bennett for establishing a virtual, yearlong writing community that supported my nascent efforts, and provided a rich and varied resource I could rely on. In addition, I must give credit—and thanks from the bottom of my heart—to the generosity of editor and writer, Teresa

Barker, whose perceptive intelligence and warmth helped me to focus these stories, and gave me confidence that these chapters would find their way in the world.

Thank you to Jean Ryan, a true friend, who offered her literary skills and talent, and gave me solid, constructive feedback without mincing words. My sister, Cindy Whiting, also brought her sharp intellect to my pages, asking insightful questions and making suggestions (more collages!) that have made this a better book. I want to thank other family members who believed in this project, and gave me the material support to print the book in all its full-color glory: Theodore A. Whiting, Teresa Carnes Whiting, David and Anne Whiting, Ted Whiting, Jr., Paula Marshall, Karen Clausen, and Lauri Clausen. Many other friends of the studio made this book possible through their contributions, and I have set aside special pages to thank them each by name. Last, but most important of all, I want to thank my partner and "secret reader," Kris Clausen, who accompanied me on every step of this journey with her loving reliability, her openhearted sense of adventure, and hot meals I could count on in-between the work of interviewing, transcribing, and writing these chapters.

ALICE DOESN'T LIVE HERE ANYMORE

Barbara Jacobsen

Two women, two artists, two friends: imaginative, independent, irrepressible, unassuming, spontaneous, guileless, and deeply wise. Two teachers, two mentors: patient, perceptive, thoroughly encouraging, fascinated, and infatuated with the possibilities of the creative pulse. Magical midwives to what's happening now. Audrey von Hawley and Barbara Jacobsen followed their vision to form a group art studio and started a movement—calling it, simply, "collage class."

When Audrey and Barbara began to explore ways of making art in a group, they had been friends for twenty years. Both had rich backgrounds in various art forms, and had lived or worked as members of The Art Farm, an art community in Sonoma, California. Each had experience as a teacher and founder of alternative schools when their own children were growing, so taking the leap to start a place for group learning was already in their blood. "We posted flyers around town, and asked people we knew to join us," Audrey recalls. "We started with collage as our medium right away because Barb was familiar with it. Mainly, when we took the studio, we needed to pay the rent, so we did classes. We were half doing it for the students, half doing it for ourselves."

Barbara had practiced drawing and painting as a young woman, including portraits of her children. Her late husband, Ray Jacobsen, a painter, encouraged her to "go for it," to become an artist. "Working with Ray was a great collaboration,"

Barbara says, fondly remembering his steady presence. "He was so supportive. I learned from him—about composition, about light and shadow. It was because of him I started to pursue painting and drawing full time."

Barbara first discovered collage one day as she was working on a drawing that was very technical. "The center of the drawing got screwed up, so I cut it out and pasted a photo of clouds and sky in the middle. I was blown away by it! That's how I started to collage—it began as an accident. That's what collage is, in a way, accidental and surprising. I fell in love with it."

It was no accident that Barbara and Audrey launched their dream after completing an intensive, yearlong workshop called *The Four-Fold Way*®[1] with teacher and mentor Angeles Arrien. Arrien's work draws from the practice of shamanic traditions of living in harmony and balance—with both the environment and one's own inner nature. She identifies four archetypes and teaches that these mythic symbols are the roots of the human family, which could offer us wisdom to live our lives.

"Angie's workshop was a launcher for me to claim my own authority," Audrey says. "It also helped me with speaking in front of people. I always say 'Barb's the teacher, and I'm the preacher!' Did we know we were starting a movement? No!" she says, laughing. "We have been called the Transformers of Sonoma, though. But in the old days everyone just made stuff. Everyone can do art. Everyone is creative. When I took part in the *Four-Fold Way*, it turned me on to my authentic self. I realized how much creativity meant to me. That's when I was able to say 'I want to be an artist.'"

Audrey is the daughter of two commercial artists who rendered advertising layouts and illustration for department stores in Manhattan, so art was a big part of her life from the start. She says she "drew all the time, from when I could hold a pencil." She and her brother listened to the Lone Ranger on the radio, and drew while the show was on. "I have notebooks full of drawings," she says, and then explains, "I was supposed to be a commercial artist, but I wanted to live in a small town, and I couldn't decide between fine art and commercial art, so I let it go. I went to college at Oberlin for two years, but I was really living out my adolescence. It was the beatnik times. I was being a beatnik, being bad."

CREATRIX

Audrey von Hawley

*That's when I was able to say,
"I want to be an artist."*

FUTURE DREAM

Barbara Jacobsen

*I saw Barbara Jacobsen's work. It was so magical, mystical, and deep.
I wanted to do collages just like those.*

Every child is an artist. The problem is

how to remain an artist once he grows up.

Pablo Picasso

Audrey never imagined that one day she would discover collage, and a destiny in creating the collage studio and the community that has grown around it.

In the early days at the studio, Barbara and Audrey taught a variety of collage techniques. They provided all the materials for collaging, including tapes and glues, scissors and knives, mat board for mounting and framing, and a variety of magazine and calendar images.

"At the beginning, we felt we needed to teach technique," Barbara says. "I loved showing people the tricks of collage. It gave me lots of fulfillment. We were also nervous at first, and felt we needed to teach. But then we backed off and became more confident as we realized that the artists were actually more successful when they found a way that worked best for them. We just encouraged them to jump in, offering our help when asked. There has been so much soul food from all this, so much gratification watching people emerge, seeing them make discoveries."

Sometimes parents can be thoughtless, condescending or even critical in their responses to a child's art. "That happened to so many of us," Audrey says, with dismay. "But now, being praised in collage, we see the art just gets better and better. When we started exhibiting collage publicly, the quality of the work evolved every year. People began to take themselves seriously and that has raised the level of the whole group."

The first public show, held as an outdoor garden event in 1995, featured art by fifteen collage artists, along with writers who read from their own published and unpublished works. The exhibit was an outgrowth of work being done at Barbara and Audrey's collage studio, as well as other independent artists practicing in Sonoma. It generated interest in collage as an emerging art medium in the valley, and promoted the Monday classes at the studio. The Sonoma Collage Collective, the independent group of artists that grew out of that collaboration, continues to exhibit work around Northern California.

"I've done lots of shows, and I still show art and do commissions, but not as often," Barbara admits. "This group work is more meaningful. Part of what I like about collage is that I've learned so much more about myself. I like the playfulness of it, almost like a mystery to solve. It can be fun and light-hearted, even though it may lead to profound insights. My favorite activity as a child was sitting on the floor arranging objects to create scenarios and stories."

Reading Jungian analyst Robert A. Johnson's books in the early 1990's further inspired Barbara to try working with collage through active imagination. In his book *Inner Work*,[2] Johnson introduces a four-step approach to work with the power of imagination, which psychologist Carl Jung developed early in the 19TH century. When Barbara applied some of Johnson's techniques to images in her collages, they sprung to life, revealing layers of possibilities. Excited with her discoveries, she began to introduce these practices into the studio work.

"I don't think we knew the collage studio would have this kind of impact when we started," Audrey says of the thousands of pieces of artwork created over the studio's thirteen-year history. "Seeing what has unfolded has blown my mind! It's just neat to know that our motivations and desires have evolved into this." Barbara voices the principles guiding her studio work without hesitating: "To be true to myself and my creativity, to enjoy my process and to share it with others. To explore more, uncover more, to always be learning, finding out what's behind the images. To reveal my life journey and the journey that connects me with everybody else. It's not just my world—I'm tapping into something that's bigger than me."

"I love colors, shapes, and stories," Audrey says. "To collage is to gather color, shapes, and textures to tell a story. Most often I find the collages tell me about my feelings in the moment, my dreams in the future, and my concerns about the state of the earth."

Establishing the collage studio with the skills, strengths, and talents the artists brought to the table introduced enormous potential. As they pooled their

CHILD'S PLAY

Barbara Jacobsen

Collage can be fun and light-hearted,
even though it may lead to profound insights.

LONG WINTER

Audrey von Hawley

*Most often, the collages tell me about my feelings in the moment,
my dreams in the future, and my concerns about the state of the earth.*

resources, learned from each other, and trusted the deeper currents of intuition, a larger work began to unfold. An interesting alchemy bubbled up over time and the combined effect of the experience has become greater—much greater— than the sum of the parts. Because of their commitment to follow their vision, Barbara Jacobsen's and Audrey von Hawley's creative community has grown and blossomed, nurturing the progress and artistic expression of the many individuals who find sustenance there. Even if you have never been part of a group circle, never tried your hand at art, you are about to drop in on just such an experience through the pages of this book—and the candid, colorful, and sometimes poignant reflections shared by the people you are about to meet. This is how their stories— and this special story of community—begin.

RETURN

Barbara Jacobsen

"You can start hanging your collages on the whiteboard," Audrey said, announcing the time. "Does anybody need to leave early?" Real time collapsed. I felt myself transported back to junior high school where I heard my art teacher calling my name, calling me to her desk to critique my figure drawing. I had stumbled on something sticking out into the aisle, and had fallen flat on the chalky tiles. As I collected myself and my artwork and continued to my teacher's desk, I was the center of attention in this room full of twelve-year-old classmates. I heard their tittering even before Miss Harper started in on her criticism of my work. But I could handle it; after all, I had a sturdy ego and a playful sense of humor. I merely blushed and grinned, slouching by Miss Harper's desk. After a long inspection, and an equally long silence, Miss Harper delivered her verdict: "Well…the head is good." Ouch! My classmates' snickering ricocheted off the slate surface of the blackboard behind me and hit me harder than I expected.

Now, thirty-two years later, I had gathered the courage to attend my first collage art class at a private studio in Sonoma, California. Excited to play hooky from work on that afternoon, I drove to class with little butterflies tingling in my gut. I didn't know who or what to expect, but I was determined to keep an open mind.

I arrived at the studio to find several artists chatting together while unpacking works-in-progress. Barbara greeted me and told me Audrey would arrive soon to conduct my orientation. Audrey gave me the complete tour in a brisk, but cheerful five minutes. Magazines and calendars swelling with photo images were filed by categories: architecture, nature, science, travel, and the like. A cutting station at the end of the studio housed rulers and straightedges, a variety of blades, and a paper cutter. Scissors, X-acto knives, glues, and tapes rounded out the tools available at the center of the work table.

That completed my orientation. If I had any questions, I could ask. Audrey reminded me not to cut the table, to please use a piece of cardboard under my knife. No lessons had been planned, and there were no techniques or craft taught that day. I didn't see any teaching going on at all. Perhaps I'd made a mistake? But I remembered the orange flyer clearly advertising collage classes. I mused about this as I made myself look busy. What the heck was I supposed to do?

I resorted to behaviors I'd learned in school—I'd find out what was expected of me and try to produce it. I settled on creating a pleasing visual image with a central theme. Yes, that's what I'd do. I jumped up with renewed confidence and strode over to the magazines. As I began looking them over, images began to stir my imagination, but then stumped me as each new image snagged my attention. *Oh…my…God!* There were literally hundreds of magazines, and thousands of images. How would I find anything that made sense in this blizzard of paper? I felt dizzy and hot, and a little annoyed.

This class was turning out to be a disaster, but I muddled through. I got a few ideas by looking around, then began to mimic what I saw in other collages. After an excruciating two-and-a-half hours, I had managed to paste several images and words into a pastiche that looked like something I'd made in junior high. Although secretly frustrated, outwardly I managed to keep my cool, hoping no one noticed my discomfort.

Then Audrey announced we could put our collages up on the whiteboard. What? We were going to *display them and discuss them?* Foiled again! I had already planned to slink out of here and never come back. Blood pounded in my inner ear, obliterating all sound. I braced for humiliation.

But then something astonishing happened: my classmates were kind. No one laughed. No one judged my silly little artwork. Barbara asked me to talk about it. "Tell us about your collage," she prompted. I managed to stammer something, then stopped. I had no idea where to begin. "Just tell us why you selected the images, or what they mean to you," she coaxed, gently.

I had no reasons why I selected these pictures. They just seemed to look vaguely arty together. I had cut out a picture frame, and inside the frame had inserted a photo of cupped hands holding a little egg. Clockwise around this central image, I'd pasted a photo of a dollar bill on fire, and a larger photo of an ecstatic young woman's face covered with glitter paint. I taped the words, "I was supposed to chant it in the morning" across her image, and then added an angel with wings, placing her as if she were watering the egg from an Evian bottle.

"What does the egg represent to you?" Barbara asked. My fledgling business popped into my mind, so I blurted that out. The greeting card company I'd launched a few years prior was struggling, but showed promise. Now my classmates knew I had my own business, which made me feel a little better, since I was clearly no artist.

"What does the dollar bill represent, and why is it on fire?"

"My business is very capital-intensive and burns up lots of money," I responded, laughing a little. But it was true.

"Who is the girl, and what is she doing?"

"The girl is me," I said, starting to feel more comfortable with this exercise in bringing meaning to something created without intention. I explained that I chanted—more likely, prayed—the same thing every morning: give me the heart and the nerve to persevere and make my business a success. Finally Barbara asked about the angel. I ventured a thought that perhaps it was my guardian angel, or a spirit guide who seemed to be nurturing my efforts with the life-giving water.

My classmates listened with respectful attention as I animated my story by responding to Barbara's prompts. Although I felt a bit self-conscious during this exploration of my artwork, I never felt judged. I have to admit, I didn't expect to

have my innermost hopes and fears revealed by pasting these random images.
I also didn't expect to be drawn into such intimacy with these strangers. Yet it was an unexpected comfort to be seen this way, without judgment. My journey suddenly became more important through their regard.

Everyone's collage received the same respect as we worked our way around the whiteboard where we'd displayed our work. Each artist was able to express or reveal as much as they chose. Then that part of the session ended and the class came to a close. I felt a gentleness in the room, and a brief silence floated aloft before the hum and pulse of individual conversations started up again. It was as if we were all witness to something fleeting and fragile, yet not completely sure it had happened at all.

a world of collage

Creating a work of art by assembling and gluing paper, fabrics, string, or other materials to a surface appears deceptively simple. Incorporating bits and pieces of commercially printed images into compositions may seem facile, yet the results for beginners and experts alike can be deeply satisfying. Fine artists Georges Braque and Pablo Picasso introduced the art of collage around 1909. The technique was developed further by artists of the Dada and Surrealist movements to include found objects, and is now linked forever to the idea of modern art. Today, any material fixed to a surface can be called collage. For now, let's dive into the experience of practicing the art of collage for personal growth using a method that Audrey von Hawley and Barbara Jacobsen have mentored for more than ten years at the Sonoma Collage Studio.

Practicing collage using Barbara and Audrey's process taps into unconscious thoughts, feelings, and patterns through a series of artistic choices. Working with pictures, we can bypass the intellect, essentially moving it aside to go to a deeper level. The very act of collaging brings us into the present, into our inner worlds, where we most easily encounter imagination. The steps we practice bring these elements into focus: how an artist chooses images, creates a composition, and attempts to find meaning in the resulting artwork through dialoguing and active imagination. The gestalt of this method of dialoguing and activating imagination

THE SCREAM

Lindsay Whiting

*Collage puts me in touch with deep thoughts and feelings
I didn't even know I had.*

PLENTY

Audrey von Hawley

*The community Barbara and Audrey have fostered
has become a comforting, nourishing one.*

is a key element to understanding the process. You'll soon see how this works as we spend some time talking with the individual artists and looking at their work.

In my six years of practice, I've been amazed at the transformational power of collage to put me in touch—literally—by choosing images, clipping them out, and arranging them in a composition—with deep thoughts and feelings I wasn't even aware I had. At first I felt self-conscious about my collages, as I had come to the studio with no real art training, but soon realized there's no need to have lots of instruction or background to make a collage. The tools are easy to find and easy to use. Old magazines are everywhere, begging to be recycled. And the quality of the experience is in the physical activity, the creative expression, and the reflection and conversation about the resulting collage.

Leafing through magazines looking for images in my first classes, I wasn't sure what to look for, and didn't know how to build a composition. Even making a simple piece of pleasing artwork seemed a challenge, since I couldn't find the images I saw in my mind's eye. Yet, the elements of meaningful coincidence and the pictures we're attracted to are actually what make the collage process so exciting, expressive, and richly rewarding.

At the studio we work alongside and across from each other at a very large, elevated table at which we can either stand or sit on high stools. Most times we chat as we begin looking through magazines, snipping and cutting images as we go. Someone suggests a good film, another tells about a book they've read. Another returns from traveling and shares photos. Sometimes an artist will come into class with a deep sadness or a problem they've been struggling with. There is true sharing as we create collages that express our lives. We are a tribe now, like family, where anything might happen, and everything is accepted.

The community that Barbara and Audrey have fostered at the studio has become a comforting, nourishing one for many of us who practice there. These kinds of places that we enjoy and tune into on a regular basis—outside of our families—offer another way for people to come together. We attend them frequently because we thrive off the energy there. The term "third place," coined by sociologist Ray Oldenburg,[3] reflects our attachment to these crucial community places. Oldenburg says third places are important to community as separate, informal gathering places and fulfill the need for affiliation that home and work—the first two places—cannot meet. They make people feel comfortable, and they nourish the need for friendship and human contact.

Most of us have a third place in our lives. It could be a local café where you hang out, or perhaps a hair salon or barbershop. Some folks join clubs. I love spending time in bookstores, so for me a bookstore with comfortable chairs is heaven on earth. In societies older than the United States, it seems there are more solid traditions of these kinds of community spaces, from the piazzas in Italy to the pubs in Ireland and England, the teahouses in Japan, the marketplaces of France, and the bazaars of Marrakech and Istanbul.

How have Barbara and Audrey managed to foster this sense of a third place— this sense of community? How have they woven such a delicate thread between us, seemingly without trying? As the founders of the studio, they somehow intuitively anchor the group, holding the space. They envisioned and recognized its importance by taking responsibility to provide this studio for the community's sake. What started from a small seed grew into a lovely garden—providing beauty and sustenance enjoyed by many.

dreaming a life

Autumn leaves crunch underfoot as I cross the little stone bridge leading to the studio. I spy both Barbara's and Audrey's cars in the parking lot. They usually arrive an hour before the students to prepare the workspace for us. When I enter the studio for class, it feels like home. Fresh new magazines beckon from the center of the table— someone has come by with a donation since the last class. These are the ones we'll look through first. Padded work stools of varying heights surround the sturdy work table to accommodate any artist who might come to collage. I look to see if works-in-progress hang on the whiteboard, or if leftover collages languish there. News articles, unusual photographs, books on craft and technique, videos, and second-hand novels are some of the many resources we find at the studio.

Each session begins with this repeated ritual: one by one, artists arrive, greeted by a welcome from Barbara, Audrey, and whoever is present, then we choose our seats and arrange our tools. It always makes me smile to myself, because I think of the TV program *Cheers*, when Norm walks into the bar and everyone calls his name.

A core group of artists has collaged at the studio since its foundation, interspersed with others who come and go. These regular artists seem to serve as a kind of yeast that inspires and excites the group. The atmosphere is uplifting, yet hard to describe. "It's an ideal situation," one artist observes. "Barbara and Audrey don't approach with criticism. They're interested, and their interest encourages people. They both give of themselves generously. You feel that. Barbara and Audrey just set good examples."

On most Mondays now, you'll find me with my tribe, my people, happily snipping and cutting, trusting myself to find my way. Out beyond our studio, the world passes by in flashes, a reminder of the hard-driving pace imposed by bruising schedules and techno-gadgets that we've chosen to leave behind, for the deeper connection of friendship and the rewards of sharing time together.

This idea of deep community isn't new. *The Book of Changes (I Ching)*, an ancient text created by the Chinese to understand the mysteries of everyday life, draws our attention to it as well. In one of the versions, interpreter R.L. Wing writes: "The planet is covered with communities, each with histories, traditions, customs, freedoms and limitations. They are communities of towns and cities, communities of career and special interests, religious and philosophical communities, or communities of racial or familial ties. They all run very deeply through time and space, and all share common experiences that bond them intricately within themselves."[4]

I know these communities exist as I have savored periods in my life when I felt part of a family or a group that gave me a sense of belonging. Yet I know that it's not love that I'm missing—I've had a loving partner for over twenty years. I also have a warm and loyal circle of friends, so I know it isn't the desire for friendship that fuels this longing. I've come to understand that love and friendship won't fill this need. Perhaps the gap so many of us feel in our lives can only be filled by this third place.

The studio creates this experience of community through a confluence of creative exploration, art and design, community, common purpose, self-expression, therapy, and spiritual practice. Collage is an extremely elastic medium that can contain and mirror back anything a practitioner puts into it. Most times this happens without effort, without intention. It happens through the unseen workings of the unconscious mind, while the conscious mind is focused somewhere else. For me, as for most of us, it happens despite what we are thinking, and it unfolds from a place deep within, apart from any effort to make it happen.

A couple of years ago I made my first truly satisfying collage, which reflected some strong feelings and moved me to a new level of composition. It felt like a breakthrough in my ability to compose an image, as all the pieces came together as a whole. Better results were beginning to emerge from practice over time. I kept that piece separate from my growing pile of collages, which I stored in a box, covering it with tissue paper for protection. I contemplated this collage often, staging it in a place where I could look at it every day. Little did I know there was a seed germinating in that image that would soon sprout, causing me to embark on a new chapter in my life.

The collage, which I call *Reverie*, is a picture of a woman in repose, dreamily gazing up at what seems like a scene from her imagination. She envisions a herd of wild horses charging across the landscape of her mind, while a huge book floats underneath, serving as a backdrop for a little boy who makes shadow puppets fly across its pages. A girl costumed as a butterfly perches on a corner of the big book, looking directly at the viewer with an enigmatic smile. The entire background is a wall of red and orange flame.

When I made the collage, I liked it right away. It expressed so many feelings that I held inside, both familiar and surprising. It gave full flight to the playful side of my imagination, and also reflected the passion I felt about my own creativity, child-like joy, and my love for books and reading.

But that wasn't the end of it. One day Barbara Jacobsen handed me a brochure for a yearlong writing workshop. I had never talked about writing and at the time wasn't writing much at all, except for some short marketing blurbs for my business. Yet somehow this simple, synchronistic event set off a chain reaction, sprouting the seed planted by my collage. Within hours, I knew that I wanted to write a book about this group art experience.

That's the way the collage process works for me. It serves to relax my mind, to ease me from the daily grind of left brain analysis to a floating world where the right brain takes flight and makes connections without really trying. When

REVERIE

Lindsay Whiting

*Little did I know there was a seed
germinating in that image...*

BETWEEN TWO WORLDS

Lindsay Whiting

Perhaps new cognition is gestating,
waiting to be discovered.

I do this collage practice, I also find my mind can access unacknowledged parts of myself, can achieve greater contact with my unconscious thoughts and feelings. The work provides a new way of knowing, which was not previously available. Through collage, we are able to bring old and new feelings to the surface to examine them, name them, and turn them into allies. There have been many instances over the years of collaging where forgotten memories or feelings were rekindled. Many times when we hang our work on the whiteboard, what another artist observes in the work can also stir up unexpected feelings, and can help us forge new connections.

There's a seemingly random, yet critical activity involved in finding and choosing images that will make up the final collage. The aesthetic and emotional resonance with the images acts like a magnet, drawing us in. That's the really exciting part. Meaning can be deciphered from the moment of creation, the personal, symbolized meanings of the images, the relationships between the images, the psychic state of the creator, and the gestalt of the parts. Instead of language driving the process, we begin with the more subjective, emotionally laden images, and work toward articulating our experiences.

From the beginning, like everyone else at the studio, I simply went along with the process; I let it take me over. I leafed through magazines and let my mind and my gaze wander. In my first collage the composition wandered too! It didn't have a focal point. With no formal art training, I hadn't worked on tonal values, scale, or any of the other established design rules. The final piece wasn't aesthetically pleasing, but the elements surprised me.

At the end of that first class, when my turn came to talk about my collage, I didn't know what to say, hadn't had this type of dialogue before. Barbara offered prompts—a few questions to engage active imagination: first, naming the pictures in the collage, then working with each one to understand these as personal symbols through the associations I made to them, and how they connected to the other images to tell a story. Barbara worked with me to help me talk about my collage to discover what it might reveal. She asked about the different images. What does the egg represent? Why is the dollar bill on fire? Who is the girl chanting in the morning? As I answered the questions, I was able to uncover what each picture meant to me and literally pieced together a story of my life—some of it unknown, even to me. And yet upon uncovering this narrative, I recognized it as my own.

Delighted when my pictures began to come into focus this way, I wanted to embrace the work, seeing its value right away. I needed to work on my composition and design, but what the dialogue revealed to me was pure gold. In a culture that values intellect and analytical thinking above all, our inner knowing becomes devalued, overridden by outside forces. The collage experience guides us to connect with our inner knowing, to dialogue with our inner selves through the use of imagery, which is our earliest, preverbal way of experiencing life. When we engage the imagery and ask it what we need to learn, it might seem odd at first to be "in conversation" with your own unconscious this way, but if the information we receive is of value, why not pursue it?

deep imagery

Using imagery to more fully understand our own human experience best describes what we practice through our work with collage. Craftsman, professor, and author Stephen Gallegos presents the concept of deep imagery in his many books and articles on the subject, including *Animals of the Four Windows*.[5] Gallegos' ideas expand on Jung's classic work on the four functions of consciousness: thinking, feeling, sensation, and intuition.[6] But in contrast to Jung, Gallegos asserts that deep imagery is the fourth function, and not intuition as Jung postulated. Instead, Gallegos presents intuition as a tool we can use to access all the other functions. Deep imagery is mysterious, and although we may try to manipulate it, we can learn to discern the differences between the organic arising of images from the inner self, and our more conscious versions of memory and fantasy. Knowing through deep imagery is drawn from the inner life, and it can lead us back to a healthier relationship with our authentic selves.

Visual images short-circuit the intellect, move it aside to go to a deeper level. Using images to tell a story through collage can reveal things over time that may not be evident at first. For example, I've made collages that seemed a bit strange, or even violent. I wondered what they were saying about the condition of my psyche! Then, weeks or even months later, I would suddenly make a connection to the artwork. In some cases, actual events occurred that revealed information linking back to a collage I'd made. The synchronicities have been uncanny. Our projections (attributing one's own feelings or attitudes onto someone or something outside oneself) are indeed valuable. To be able to see them mirrored in our work, or in our everyday actions is the reality of our lives—often the somewhat hidden reality. I believe it is through our projections that we discover ourselves, and that we can realize immense power when we acknowledge we are truly co-creators of our worlds.

The following stories are my reasons for writing this book. Each of the artists who has done this work at the studio has a story and a journey of inner discovery. In the telling, we'll hear the artists speak from their own experience. In a way, it is a taste of the studio's trademark dialoguing process. In this case, however, it is the Sonoma Collage Studio experience itself that is on display, and the dialogue in the pages ahead reveals the rich and diverse ways each artist's life has been profoundly affected by it. My hope is that whether you are an accomplished collage artist or simply curious about the art or the way it can change your life, you'll find a satisfying blend of wonder and wisdom awaiting you in the art and conversations you find here.

A FINE BALANCE

Phyllis Finney

Why are you perched so precariously there?

"How can you *feel* a color?" Phyllis asks. She closes her eyes, sitting in the home that's been in her family for decades, framed by watercolors and acrylic paintings that cover the living room walls. "Well, when I'm playing Brahms on the violin, I feel browns and yellows, mostly warm colors because Brahms is such a romantic, earthy composer. Now let's take Mozart. His music is blue—and green like crisp lettuce. Very clean sounding. The intonation has to be absolutely perfect or it's nothing."

Phyllis pauses to put more coffee on to brew and to steep tea for herself. She moves nimbly about the kitchen, from the fridge to the stove, and apologizes for not knowing the proper proportions to make coffee. At eighty-four, Phyllis has a meticulous memory for details and her bright eyes glisten and widen as she rattles off references to music, geography, history, and literature.

Phyllis played violin with a symphony orchestra for more than twenty years until arthritis in her hands prevented her from reaching the high performance standards she'd come to expect of herself. Retirement from the music world had left a void where her art quickly took root and bloomed. When Phyllis' neighbor told her about the collage studio, Phyllis started coming to classes on Mondays as often as she could. "I went to collage only to make art," Phyllis says. "I didn't know it was going to go this deep." Her interactions with other students at the studio, along with their personal stories, moved her in a way that other art classes had not. Painting classes she had taken had focused only on tools, materials, and technique. "It's the connections that are really important in life. One has to be connected, not isolated."

The first studio where Phyllis attended Barbara and Audrey's collage class was an inexpensive rental—a converted garage that the two collaborators had found to house their dream. Tucked away off the street at the back of a group of small apartments, it provided a place to seat artists, to set up the huge table with supplies, and to shelve the growing numbers of magazines and collage images.

"The classes haven't changed much since then," Phyllis says. "Except gradually—or maybe I just became aware—there was more dialoguing or whatever you'd say about the group process. My participation level changed. That last half hour was always the whiteboard where we display our art. Barbara and Audrey began to urge people to get more in touch with their collage by asking us, 'What are you trying to say? How are you connected to the art?' That's when we took the experience from art critiquing to dialoguing. The students wanted it. Through time, most students got more sophisticated with art, composition, values, and balance too."

How does Phyllis approach the process of collage? What is her state of mind and what are her feelings as she creates her compositions?

"I don't approach the work intellectually. I just put things down artistically, when things suddenly pop out at me. They are done unconsciously." Phyllis bends over her collage work with quiet concentration, letting most of the chatter in the group pass by like high, lacy clouds. Occasionally she lets out a sharp, hilarious observation, *sotto voce*. She thumbs through magazines provided at the studio but sometimes brings images that she feels are beautiful or provocative. She rarely has a specific goal in mind, but more importantly to her, strives to keep the composition and tonal values true to some deeper attunement with the emerging piece.

Phyllis starts with five or six images most times, and then she begins to assemble them as a composition. When she's not able to integrate the pieces or when her thoughts are scattered, she tends to go abstract, to let go into the outrageous. "The plan isn't working, so I go crazy. Some of my best collages are those!"

But what's the difference between having a planned composition and going crazy as Phyllis suggests? What are her feelings that tell her the plan is falling apart? "Well, always, composition is important. It must be artistically balanced," she says.

Phyllis' relationship to art is intricately woven with her family history, beginning with a bit of serendipity at the age of nine. She remembers a man coming to the door of her family home, an entrepreneur launching a music school. He recruited students by asking "Would you like to play the piano or the violin?" Since Phyllis' mother played the piano, she thought if Phyllis played the violin they could play together. As Phyllis' skills advanced, the accompaniment became too difficult for her mother, though Phyllis' story was just beginning. Her parents got season tickets to the symphony and as Phyllis was growing up, she was also exposed to other art forms.

Her father was a commercial sign painter who had mastered the rare and painstaking art of gilding using gold leaf. Her mother loved to draw and had always wanted to go to art school, but her dream was deferred when her own mother died. Both of Phyllis' parents fully supported her violin lessons. Art—or being accomplished in some kind of art—was revered in their household and Phyllis was the only child; she carries that reverence with her today.

In the collage studio, artists work with color, form, composition, and texture as well as their relationships to the whole. "One can use the same terms in music," Phyllis says. "They all overlap. For example, let's take color. Mahler's music is deep purple because purple is a rich, intense color. But Mahler is full of surprises too. At first you might hear a conglomerate of colors; they're all mixed up. Then suddenly a beautiful blue sky comes out, a beautiful melody. An ultramarine blue."

Phyllis says she can't play Debussy without thinking of the Impressionist painters. She "sees" bits of color that make up the vibrations totally unique to the Impressionists. It's the way Debussy composed that makes her feel this way. "It's not literal, but subjective and evocative—like squinting at a solid form."

Phyllis views composition the same way; that there has to be a form to the art, form to the music. And there has to be balance—the way the parts are organized must be pleasing to the ear or to the eye. There could be some surprises too, but they should be balanced with the whole. That's very important to Phyllis when she works on her art. It's visceral to her. She's not happy with her work unless it's satisfying to her, personally.

"In music, why is the diatonic scale there?" Phyllis asks. "Because it's our natural scale. Then when you change it to a minor scale, that's the surprise element. It changes it, but the music is still confined within the octave."

When Phyllis first began creating collages and worked on design concepts, she had a terrible time being abstract—everything turned into a realistic picture. Now she's trying to get away from realism. She'll take a realistic image and cut it into interesting shapes, or she'll use blocks of color cut into pieces to change the form.

"Take this one for instance. I cut out an abstract figure, a black figure, then I added color. Next I selected cool colors to paste over warm colors. I used the same shapes—wavy shapes—I cut them out and put them down. Just the beguess and the begosh. Then you start to see things. I hadn't started to dialogue yet, but I tried to write about the artwork."

digging down

The process Phyllis mentions—dialoguing—comes at the end of each collage class, usually in the last half hour. That's when each artist hangs her or his finished collage or work-in-progress on the expansive whiteboard that extends along one side of the studio. After several calls from Audrey, we finally, almost grudgingly, comply with most of us still working, trying to put finishing touches on our pieces.

We hang our art then, whatever we've completed or want to put up on the wall. We display the pieces, discuss them, and sometimes dialogue with our artwork. Everyone's collage gets the same treatment. We can say as little or as much as we want to about our finished collages, or about our process as it unfolded that day. Our classmates will sometimes make observations, yet it is understood that our discussions don't take the form of critiquing.

Although we are creating works of art, the emphasis at the studio is more on our process and individual level of participation, not on publicly exhibiting our

> The primary benefit of practicing any art, whether well or badly,
>
> is that it enables one's soul to grow.
>
> *Kurt Vonnegut Jr.*

art or becoming commercial artists. The feedback is most productive when our classmates merely make observations about the work, essentially holding up a mirror reflecting how they see each piece, so that each artist can integrate the feedback at his or her own pace. We rarely tell each other how to fix a collage or make it better, unless an artist has a specific question about their own composition. The depth and quality of disclosure in this process is a sensitive balance, a special magic, which makes the studio so beloved among the artists.

"As for dialogue in studio work, I don't do too well with it," Phyllis admits. "I hadn't really sat down on my own to do it. Maybe I'm self-conscious. It can be very revealing. Just looking at anything in the picture, and talking to it, to ask why it's there, why it's important to you. This is a kind of hang-up for me. I was able to do this one pretty well. I call it *A Fine Balance*." Phyllis shows her artwork and gives an example of her dialogue: "Why are you perched so precariously there...?" Her voice trails into silence. She was still thinking about it, not wanting the dialogue to be contrived.

In *A Fine Balance* there's lots of texture, and rhythm too. The rigid lines of the fence and the relaxed curvy lines are in counter-rhythm and there's movement in the deeper background texture.

"The woman on the fence is balancing, teetering," Phyllis explains. "There's movement with her. Looking back at this collage, I'd say I had doubts. I had ambivalence about the way my life was going. It was a matter of giving myself permission to speak out about things, and also to change my mind if I felt like it. My own mother used to say, 'I'm eighty-five, I can say whatever I want to!' That's what's happening to me. That's what the fine balance is—it's between being sensible and being a little bit daring. I speak up now."

For Phyllis, the dialogue comes from great emotional depth. She figures it emerges as an association with something that has happened to her in her life—perhaps a sweet, sad, traumatic, or shocking experience. "No, wait, that's not totally true…some are about children," Phyllis says, reconsidering. "I'm agonizing over this." She had been overwhelmed by the great numbers of children in poverty worldwide, and pulls out another collage to illustrate her point. "This is not within my experience, but I see it in the newspapers and the news. I call it *Beyond Reach*. These children in this collage are trying to reach food, the beseeching, reaching hands of children." Phyllis reads a partial dialogue about the plight of these children, concluding, "Our hearts must answer."

It's true that many times we come to the studio with daily worries about our families and loved ones, the state of the country, natural disasters, about wars in various parts of the world. Inevitably these issues make it into our collages, providing an outlet for our frustrations, anger, and fear at the conditions we see around us. The very act of creating becomes a counterbalance against the violence and disintegration, our way of re-visioning our world.

"It's the deep emotional feeling that distinguishes the difference between contrived versus authentic dialogue," Phyllis explains. "I have a hard time dialoguing immediately, before it sinks in. When I wake up in the morning I say my form of prayers and meditate, sometimes things come then. My mind is fairly clear. It's without any other distracting thoughts. I'm just waking up. I remember my dreams, and I think about them. What's Jung's word for it—tribal memory, collective unconscious? I think that's what dreams are.

"I don't want to get self-conscious while I'm collaging." Phyllis strives to put images together as a visual artist, and then she looks at what comes later. She feels she can be subtly aware that meanings may emerge, but puts that aside, letting them come in their own time.

"After I put images down, I may discover meaning. On this one, *Beyond Reach*, I found the hungry boy first. Then I found the petroglyphs, the hands. I thought,

BEYOND REACH

Phyllis Finney

I found the hungry boy first, then the petroglyphs.
I thought,"This goes with that"—I saw it, I felt it.

THE BLUE GUITAR

Phyllis Finney

I was inspired by Wallace Stevens' poem,
The Man with the Blue Guitar.

'The boy goes with the petroglyphs.' I saw it. I felt it. I consciously recognized the deep dialogue between these images—an emotional connection. Now we look at it and say, 'Longing and pies and hands.' What do those hands represent to me? They are yearning. They are not grasping, but pleading. They are hands of children in want. And they need help. There's a shift that occurs, going from visual motif to the dialogue, an association. And as symbols for instance, they're not personal, but universal."

Next, Phyllis pulls out the collage she calls *The Blue Guitar*, inspired by Wallace Stevens' poem *The Man with the Blue Guitar*.[7] She remembers a class with a Dominican nun who used the poem as a metaphor to teach about the life of Christ: "It was my feeling about it. I used the symbol of the snake to signify life and death, resurrection, reincarnation, nirvana, a leaping into paradise. I wanted to make something that expressed the poem."

the symbolic life

The collage experience can be a very personal journey. Students come to class unsure of the process, unaware of working with collage as a way toward personal growth and a spiritually engaged life—most assume it will follow the more typical format of technique and critique. Yet the result is that many of us come to a deeper relationship with the process—and with ourselves. Playing in the fields of the conscious and unconscious mind puts a spotlight on the treasures we get to consider: feelings and events that have passed and are long buried, or perhaps new cognition that has been gestating, waiting to be discovered.

Doing any work to mine ore from the unconscious serves to exercise our intuition. Almost anything that is a projection is true for that moment. Like a Rorschach, which can be examined and construed, almost anything can be read or interpreted. It's up to us to begin to understand our own personal symbols to learn how to work with them. Phyllis expressed her deep, spiritual feelings in *The Blue Guitar* and uncovered her grief about child poverty in creating *Beyond Reach*.

All these methods are exercises in knowing, in honing the intuitive hunch, learning to connect to meaning that may not yet be apparent. These inklings come to our conscious awareness through various symbols and events, pointing to what it is that we need to know. We are both the observers and the observed—who influence, interact with, and determine the outcome. As we apply ourselves to collage practice, even when feeling skeptical, we come to trust the process. We begin to feel and see the subtleties involved in getting the conscious mind out of the way. We begin to open the door to knowing things in a new and different way. When Phyllis practices her morning ritual of prayers and meditation, her mind is clear. Then she can remember her dreams and bring them to conscious awareness.

Psychologist C.G. Jung wrote extensively about the language of dreams and the importance of living what he called a symbolic life.[8] He mourned the loss of living rituals in our changing world, as we grew further away from our instinctual past. Giving time daily to vows and meditation fulfills the need to express the soul, Jung argued. Without ritual, the loss of soul leads to a banality, a boredom that leads people to seek ever-greater stimulation through sensation.

Think of the growing noise pollution in our public spaces, the escalating violence in the blockbuster movies we've invented, the constant ringing of cell phones, our over-consumption of food and drink, even the shallow distraction of celebrity, that all bring us further away from connecting to our own mystery. Jung proposed that to bring back a symbolic life is to fulfill one's role in the divine drama, in something bigger than ourselves.

In his lifetime, Jung had observed the rituals of the Pueblo Indians whose tribal religion had been as the Sons of Father Sun. They believed that they help Father Sun to rise daily and walk across the heaven, that it was their responsibility to perform this ritual for the entire world. They believed that without their help, Father Sun would not continue to rise. Their role in the divine drama provided them a belief in something bigger than themselves. Without these rituals, Jung said, we restlessly search for meaning. The Pueblo emphasis on kinship, community, and traditional religion survives today, with some rites and ceremonies performed in secret, while others are performed in elaborate public dances.

AD LIB

Phyllis Finney

Now that's me!

It was becoming clear that the collage process itself could perhaps meet some of our most soulful needs, might fulfill our search for meaning in this contemporary life as Jung suggested. Our engagement with the creative process becomes a point where we can connect to deep and lasting transformation. "I look at everything so differently since I've become a collagist," Phyllis says. "All of life has changed—a door opened and more light came in, a window opened and fresh air came in. It gives me new perspective on everything."

STUDIO CLIPS   Use one of your favorite magazines with diverse images for this exercise, because you'll use only this one magazine. First, select a background image of any size, with ample room to hold several more images. Now, take your time to examine pictures from various articles, ads and sidebars. Look closely at what might be available to collage. Use your imagination. After you've perused the images, hone your search, selecting the images that appeal to you most. Without asking "why," cut out four to six different images of various sizes and colors, and compose them onto your background. You can layer, cut, juxtapose, or randomly fit images together any way you like. Limit your time on this exercise to twenty minutes. Setting limits will simplify and focus your choices.

THE DAY THE DRYER BROKE

Phyllis Finney

RAVEN

Sarah O'Hala

Although I had created two other pieces first,
I knew this was the one I came to do.

Eucalyptus trees surrounding the art studio shiver and rattle a quiet, gray-green song, releasing their resinous fragrance into the morning breeze. Sunlight dapples the parking lot, repeating the patterns of the stones placed there to prevent it from turning into a muddy lake during the rainy season. Sarah walks with a slow but deliberate gait—either mindful of her steps or perhaps lost in thought—picking her way across the gravel. Turning toward the collage studio, she suddenly looks up and breaks into a huge grin.

Sarah, along with many of the artists, has her regular spot at the big collage table. It's funny how we gravitate to the same seats on a weekly basis. Although students change regularly in an open class, we are still drawn to "our" spots, returning again and again, as if by an invisible homing device. Today the soft autumn light draws her to sit near the windows, breaking her usual pattern.

"I first started coming here to the studio in 2000," Sarah says. "A colleague where I taught at an alternative school collaged here. I often noticed she would have these…*somethings*…on her desk. I was very curious about them and asked her what they were. I wanted to know how to make one, how to put one together. That was the first drop of water in the bucket."

Sarah has a teaching credential and a master's in guidance and counseling. Her educational background is heavy in the humanities, philosophy, and literature, but no art. She took a night class in life drawing once, which she enjoyed, but expresses disappointment that she hadn't explored creativity and art earlier in her life.

"Coming to this collage studio, I was plenty intimidated," Sarah admits. "I was very, very quiet for a long time. Quiet because I knew there were artists of various levels, art degree or not. I was quiet about what I could say about my collages. I was very uneasy about talking about them, or dialoguing with them."

After we've worked on our collages for a couple of hours, we hang our work on the whiteboard to talk about it or to dialogue with it. Now comes the interesting part of the class for many of the students who have been practicing at the studio for several years.

The philosophy of dialogue was conceived by Judaic scholar, teacher, and social activist Martin Buber in the early 1900's. What Buber called "I-Thou dialogue" depicts the relationship between mankind and the world, an equal relationship of direct, open interdependence (me and you, versus me and it). The ultimate relationship, he proposed, was between mankind and God, which could be known through everyday living. He taught that the essence of religious life was not a set of beliefs, but how one engages and meets the challenges of life.

Following Buber's ideas, the dialoguing practice at the studio puts the artists in relationship to their collage. We address each image in a direct and open way—not as a thing, but as a "thou," equal to ourselves. What can the work tell us? What can we learn through this subjective approach?

A spontaneous answer can be very revealing, sometimes surprising. Even an untrained person can glean good information using this process. It's like talking with a friend, or writing about an issue to clarify what you think about it. But what was Sarah's hesitation around dialoguing in class?

"I think it's innately difficult for me to reveal myself, although I talk lots in worlds outside this studio with no problem at all. But when it comes to expressing the process of making the images, about what they mean or imply, or where they come from, it's difficult for me to articulate or reveal it to the group. Revealing it to the group is a tickly thing for me to do. I don't know if it's because I have that Scorpio vein in me that wants to keep it behind the scenes, to keep it secret."

Sarah also resists some of the terms people in class use to talk about their collages. She gives examples of what she calls psychobabble—phrases like "inner critic" and "inner child." She knows what they mean intellectually and how one could use those words to talk about a collage, but she resists using those kinds of terms to discuss images. She just doesn't feel they're accurate; she doesn't identify images with these words.

Others often feel leery of the process too, at first, hearing their own "inner skeptics" howling at them. Yet they are game to give this dialoguing a go, and some are lucky enough to strike gold on their first try. They discover insights about what is important in their lives, which help them to move forward. Experiencing that right from the start can be very affecting. It energizes students to do the work.

So what keeps Sarah coming back to class? If she is hesitant or perplexed by the dialoguing process, what's her motivation to keep coming back to the collage studio? Why make collages?

"I bring them home and put them in front of an altar I have, or on a windowsill. I leave them there for weeks, or months sometimes. I look at them every day. I become familiar with the figures or the symbols, and I begin to recognize them. They're telling me a story and I'm paying attention. That's when the verbal language can start."

heading to the source

Sarah makes copies of her collages, and then pastes them into a book. To help her talk about her collages, she writes about them on the opposing page. Sometimes it's just nonsense writing, but sometimes she discovers a kernel of meaning. Since she began keeping these homemade journals of her work and Barbara Jacobsen has encouraged her to write, Sarah feels more aligned with the collage. "I'm able to take it in with language up here," she says, pointing to her head. "I'm processing it with language better."

Sarah uses the word "aligned" to describe the moment she gets the kernel of meaning out of a piece. What does being in alignment with her artwork mean to her? As she begins to answer, her eyes and her voice soften, and the words roll out in one mellifluous thread: "Aah. . . to me it is utter bliss to be aligned. I've finally yielded to the yearning to have it expressed in the world. It's come out of me and I'm so glad that now I see it, because it was unexpressed inside," she says, as she points to her heart. "When it's out, it makes me feel happy, pleased, fulfilled, feeling sublime about everything, because now I can see it looking back at me."

Sarah describes her sense of alignment as "something that needs adjustment falling into place," perhaps an imbalance in the self, something buried, or a part of the psyche that has become disabling. A collage image might bring new perspective, somehow balances what's "off"—or by contrast, bring the imbalance into relief. The process itself may be uncomfortable, but nonetheless fulfilling. Something falls into place. "It may take a while," Sarah acknowledges, "but with a little push, a pull, it's a great moment to become aligned, for the collage to come into focus. My images resonate with me, yours with you. To fully see yourself in some way that you can't articulate—we have those moments that we discover in collage."

Often when Sarah's collages happen spontaneously and unconsciously, she finds it a bit unnerving. She doesn't know where it comes from, wasn't even working on that subject, she didn't have that in mind. That happens a lot in collage. Barbara and Phyllis have voiced that same notion; collages are happy accidents. Yet the answer seems to elude all of us—where do they come from?

"I think the creative life-soul exists in all of us. That mystery is…oh boy, that's hard to explain. Where does it come from?" she repeats, to give herself time to figure an answer. "Well, I guess it is part of myself, experienced or recognized through great magic or mystery," she explains. "If you think of a vortex or maybe a whirling dervish or spiral, something going around and around. Maybe that throws it out—the life force, this creative fire. It's always burning. It's always burning, but not automatic. I think we need to feed ourselves to keep the embers burning, otherwise it might go out."

Perhaps the creative life-soul points to chi, which the Taoists believe to be the vital force inherent in all things. Or maybe it matches the belief from Hinduism, that it is Shakti the mother goddess who is the source of all energy, creativity, and power. Could the fire also be Kundalini energy—the vital, life-sustaining force in the body— awakened from the base of the spine?

"All those words could describe the mystery that connects us to forces that preceded us eons ago," Sarah says. "The mystery that makes us able to have a continuity with all people, two-leggeds, and other creatures, the four-leggeds.

And beyond time, even beyond when time ceases. We are immediately and always connected with a primal force. Kundalini, yes that's okay too. But a primal life that is never-ending. I suppose it is divinity."

Sarah's Protestant upbringing was a huge influence in her early years. She was aware of the biblical teachings of her Sunday school and her grandparents were "big Bible readers" in Oklahoma. When Sarah was married for the first time, she converted to Catholicism but she says she was a terrible Catholic. She has since returned to Protestantism, but also has experienced many events with the recent death of her husband Bill, that made her think again. "Some pretty existential stuff."

The constraints of traditional religion do not put Sarah in touch with the mystery that she experiences with collage and art. It doesn't give her the chance for transformation and beauty to occur. So collage is her sacred life, her sacred invitation to connect her inside life with the outside life—the inner life that all people possess. Sarah feels it should be easier to bring those epiphanies and practices into everyday life, but somehow things get in the way.

"When I come to the studio, I'm connecting. When I walk from the car, that's the myth, I'm heading to the source," she says. "I've never experienced anything like this before, but I knew it was around. When I first saw the collages…ooh, I wanted that! There is a yearning for the primal celebration of oneself, and then to celebrate it together. Collaging is a solitary process many times, but the celebration here is collective, which I believe is the best way."

in the realm of the muses

In the life of artists, we often hear about the workings of the ethereal Muse, the invisible source of inspiration who, alone, compels them. Sarah, too, is compelled by something inside or outside of herself to express "this part of me, who I am, that I only sense when it's here," as she points to her heart.

Her words seem to mirror passages from American mythologist Joseph Campbell's work.[9] Campbell said that the realm of the Muses is where myth lives. He quotes the 18TH century poet Novalis when he tells us: "The seat of the soul is there where the inner and the outer worlds meet." Campbell believed that where these inner and outer worlds come together we find myth, and that the problem of making the two worlds meet is the function of the artist.

Campbell has influenced many artists, from filmmakers such as George Lucas and Steven Spielberg, to musicians including the Grateful Dead. His work has encouraged artists of all kinds to express the metaphors and archetypes inside the ancient myths. Campbell believed that the power of these images and icons runs very deep, that it goes down all the way to the ground of our biology as humans, but that we need to reclaim them for our times. He said we need to take the highest ideals and recreate them for ourselves.

"I love Joseph Campbell," Sarah says, enthusiastically leaning forward on the arms of her chair. "I never get tired of him." Excited, she flips through her notebook until she finds what she's looking for. "This is a Joseph Campbell quote I placed where I can see it over my desk." She clears her throat, then reads this quote aloud: "We must be willing to get rid of the life we've planned, so as to have the life that is waiting for us." Sarah savors Campbell's words, couching them in silence, then continues: "When I come here to the studio, this is the life that's waiting for me. And my life shows it. More and more now, this is my reality. Probably it's related to age, maybe life experiences, but this is my reality.

"Barbara Jacobsen has been absolutely inspirational to me, too. She listens very carefully, honoring what I say, urging me to live this life. She somehow gives me courage to live it. When I did Barbara's Journey Book workshop (collage combined with writing exercises) it was quite intense and frightening at times," Sarah admits. "Barbara allowed all that to come out, to be revealed. She is non-judgmental, so utterly encouraging. She laughs, she finds humor. She really saved my life I think—my creative life—and my life since Bill's death. Because of her…what's the word that females have—fecundity? Her fertility has been remarkable. I don't think I've known anyone like Barbara."

Sarah pulls out her portfolio to show the collages she's working on. Voicing her process in perusing the magazines, she mumbles softly to herself: *rip, rip, not too much thought, might be talking, talking, talking; rip that out; not thinking, just tearing things out, not thinking about it, rip, rip, rip….*

"I get almost hypnotized when I select images. The images beguile me, so my stack of pictures gets pretty big!" Sarah says, laughing. "I'm not really aware. It's like highway hypnosis—something else drives me." There are times when Sarah feels connected to an image, sees it immediately, then goes to the collage right then and there. Sometimes the strong feelings come first, sometimes later, but sometimes not at all. She just intuitively knows when images fit together.

At one time Sarah felt herself easily seduced by interesting or beautiful images, but now she's trying to go beyond "what's easy." Increasingly, she is tuning in to select images that she feels call to her more strongly. She's trying to stretch herself in her practice. What does it mean to have an image "call to her?" Her eyes turn toward the ceiling as she takes her time rolling this question around in her mind, perhaps recreating the kinesthetic memory of collaging.

"Because I can't put it back, I can't discard it," she says, finally. "Now to go underneath that, there are relationships between the pictures themselves. I'm thinking of the first image or maybe the second one—two images that I know go together. But how do they go together? How do I know that?"

Sarah voices the workings of a muse, or a force which guides her selection. Maybe it's intuition, or maybe a super-heightened state of awareness. "I go into a state sometimes. Sort of a zone." She says she knows it's an altered state because people hand images to her and she doesn't remember taking them. She goes into a creativity zone, what she calls a trance. Another artist told Sarah that when she sits next to her, she sometimes feels drawn into a meditative state, too. Perhaps Sarah is entraining the other artist to her vibe, her rhythm. When we're with someone who's nervous, we may suddenly feel irritated. If we're with someone who's calm or meditative, we may spontaneously feel drawn into an alpha state, we become very relaxed.

Sarah figures she makes selections out of a creative force of some kind, that is mostly intuitive. She may sometimes consciously choose images that are aesthetic and pleasing to her eye—or sometimes by theme, or color. Then there are the intuitive images. They feel *sticky*, she says; she can't "put them back." It's very freeing to let it go to serendipity, to rely on the unconscious mind to do its work. Perhaps that is truly being in the zone. "Maybe it expresses something I can't express, or it prognosticates. There is something about the image that I want, that I feel a desire for. Sometimes it takes me by surprise."

Today, Sarah shows an image that she describes as strange and weird: a woman with a cloth lantern on her head sits on a chair holding a bag. There is something in it that Sarah "had to have." She wonders what's in the bag. The figure is unrevealed at the moment. Does she have more tricks? When Sarah first saw her, she continued flipping through the magazine, but then went back to the page, finally giving in and cutting the image out.

Work of seeing is done. Now practice heart-work
upon these images captive within you.
Rainer Maria Rilke

"I don't know what that is about," Sarah admits. "But that's why I come to collage every week. It's something that has to be expressed. There are things within us that are so unsaid, so unarticulated, but they are there. This helps to say it—whatever it is—and there's something very fulfilling about getting it out, a personal satisfaction." That makes Sarah think of those artists who have collaged for five or six years or more. The process itself becomes more complex. Images and themes become more subtle, composition becomes more sophisticated, where years before the students wouldn't have done that work, but would go for the easier picture.

Sarah digs into a folder of work she has saved over five years of collage practice. She pulls one out, lays it on the table and begins to tell how it had developed. "Here's a collage that came out of a magazine article. The text was a mythical story about a girl and a stag that was very detailed, very complex. I was consciously working on sculpture and shape, and I learned lots from this, about arches and depth. Technically, it was about dimension. I didn't know how to do that before. I felt good about it, and in the process, turned the stag into a female. I turned it into my own personal myth, I rewrote it."

Sarah spreads her work out on the table, shuffling through the collages with care. The images themselves can be made up of many intricate pieces that entail very

LUNA CORAZON

Sarah O'Hala

There are things within us that are so unsaid,
so unarticulated, but they are there.

STAG

Sarah O'Hala

I was consciously working on sculpture and shape.
I learned lots from this—about arches and depth.

fine handwork. Many of the artists own specialized, tiny scissors or X-acto knives, which they bring to class. When everyone hangs their work for review, it's not unusual for people to step forward and gently run their fingers over a collage as if reading Braille. We all learn more about composition by finding out how many small images make up the finished piece.

self love is damn hard

Sarah shows a few more collages, smoothly rotating the pages, giving each a few words. Then she spots one that stops her cold. "This one is all about a dead promise," Sarah says, softly. "I call it *Self Love is Damn Hard*. Love has been ripped out." Then, almost as if talking to herself she says, "Wait, that's not supposed to happen." Then, as if to explain, "Boulders fell on her. And here's the dream part—she looks like she's electrocuted herself. Love is everything they said—not! See, look here, her two legs come out of one side of her body. She's a misfit, a circus figure. And she's no angel, despite the wings. She's in a very dark forest."

Sarah's tone is solemn. This collage had come from a very deep place. She had lost her husband to cancer and deep grief had informed this piece made after his death. The art is poignant, intense, and utterly personal. Slowly, Sarah moves on to another collage she wants to show.

"Yesterday, this one just fell together. Although I created two other pieces first, I knew this was the one I came to do—I call it *Raven*. The woman peeking out from behind the red is a woman I've used in another collage. Probably she has had an encounter with the underworld, and she's coming back up. She had to burn some of her own feathers, so to speak. But she's alive. The bird is a raven or crow, protecting the woman. I think much of this is autobiographical, parallel to my own life. After death there's always new life. I would attest to that—*I know it!*"

Sarah feels the group process is an integral part of the studio work, too. It's not enough just to make a collage. She says putting it up on the wall is a statement of each artist's heart and soul, their expression. "This is the place to honor it…Audrey and Barbara have created this place."

SELF-LOVE IS DAMN HARD

Sarah O'Hala

She's a misfit, a circus figure.
And she's no angel, despite the wings...

Sarah wants to hear what each artist says about their own work. "The mere expression is almost sacred in how it's articulated," she says. The very idea of giving voice to the collage commands Sarah's attention because of the divine process, that soul, that connection between what we do and putting it out in public. Sarah wonders how they got their images. Is it the same as mine? It wakes her up.

It seems that Sarah was listening closely, not for an art technique so much as an inner vision. She says she's learning art technique, but listens most to what others go through—what their thoughts are and how they dialogue. She wants to know what she has in common with the other artists. Perhaps the first layer, the first glimpse of the collage reveals one's current occupation, the daily experiences that are holding us now. When Sarah looks at the collages she's done in the last year, she recognizes that they're all about death! She didn't want to accept that at first, she wanted to run away from it. Yet death became the creative force.

Sarah believes there are also unseen processes that the artist can't sense immediately, which may manifest later. "If we have utter honesty, integrity, authenticity—conceive this group as utterly authentic—there may be insight from this that can give us signs, awareness, that we wouldn't access if we didn't do this work," she explains. "It's collaborative power, or divine synergy. Like a comet going around. When we're around other people outside class, I don't feel that. It's more mundane. I don't know if it's possible to live on such a high plateau after being here. But I think it's worth trying. Why not?

"I've heard candid conversations in this class that just about knocked me off my feet! You just don't talk about this stuff in public…taboos and stuff that is discouraged in the outer world. These people have seen a lot of life! I've thought, imagine if we all acknowledged our failures, our secrets out loud. What power!"

Maybe the energetic shift comes from a sense of absolution, or reconciliation with what is. Maybe by freeing up the energy around what holds us back, we feel a palpable sense of relief? "One is redeemed," Sarah affirms. "Redemption, despite defeat. Despite your circumstances." When Sarah taught Shakespeare to her school classes, they found redemption in the last act, some closure on the issues. Someone has been saved, someone has found his or her path in the forest, something has occurred that allows that character to carry on and go forth.

There's been a union of the disparate parts, and something has been gained from the experience.

"I've gained something," Sarah says. "It's a good feeling. I like it, but I'm not sure what it is! Barbara and Audrey emulate it—by letting the junk fall away. They know how to do it. I can't say they've risen above the everyday, or that they don't get tired. They just take the everyday life and still live the *real* life. They're trying to live on a higher plane, to transcend the mundane. I've seen others in our class do that too. They struggle with things like making a living, but they keep coming back to their art, to their real life."

STUDIO CLIPS   Select one of your own finished collages to try dialoguing. Pick a central image or character in your collage and try talking with it. Ask the image what it represents, ask why it is in your collage, and ask what it has to say to you. Be patient. Just allow your imagination to "make up" the answers. See if you discover any insights that may arise from your unconscious associations with these images.

MR. FOX

Sarah O'Hala

I don't know if it's possible to live on such a high plateau
after being here. But I think it's worth trying.

SACRED CIRCLE

Barbara Crow

This circle is a way to keep her safe.

From a young age, Barbara C. wanted to study art. "But my father thought it wasn't practical and I wouldn't be able to get a job," she says. Instead she majored in art history, then she laughs as she delivers the punch line: "Which was even more impractical!"

A tall woman, Barbara carries herself with quiet poise. She seems like someone you might meet at a gallery, or at an airport on her way to someplace around the world. As a young college graduate, Barbara traveled around Europe, enthusiastically viewing the art in every church and museum she could find. Back in the States, Barbara worked in print production scheduling and traffic, and discovered the collage studio through a coworker at an advertising agency.

"For me, lots of this studio work is about community—being part of a sacred circle," she explains. Barbara recently started a full-time job after many years of freelancing, interrupting her collage practice of six years. "I realize I've cut off most of my community," she says wistfully. "So much of it is connecting—with the community, with myself, with Audrey and Barbara J."

Today Barbara attended what we call open studio, a free time for collage artists to collage without Barbara and Audrey's facilitation. She didn't intend to create or finish an art piece; she just wanted to reconnect with the community. She wanted to be creating with others; to be in that milieu. She enjoys bouncing ideas and conversation off the other artists and says there's like-mindedness, cross-pollination going on. "Like going to a business meeting, or a professional group, you kibitz, you network," she explains. "It's being with your people. I don't have that anywhere else in my life, really. It reminds me—keeps it fresh in me—that I'm an artist. It keeps me grounded that I'm an artist first. I find I develop that muscle more when I'm around other artists."

Barbara feels that the circle helps her by supporting and fostering her creativity. She attributes that to feeling safe, rather than judged, at the studio. It nurtures her creativity. It's also community support that enables her to look at how far she has come in her own art. "I know I can bring my art here and show it to get feedback. That's pretty significant. Along with the cut magazine collage, I'm also a painter, and I want to do more painting with mixed media. I think other artists at the studio are doing that as well.

"I love taking art classes. I have to do it—it's in me. It's my form of expression." Barbara has always wanted to be in creative environments and around like-minded people. Whenever she has free time, she practices art and has taken many formal art classes where she has learned various art techniques. Yet she feels that coming into the collage studio is a unique experience when she compares it to the others. She finds the collage studio more welcoming, more encouraging, and more affirming than traditional art classes. She finds tremendous safety there that allows her to trust enough to go inside herself to do the inner work.

"There is this sense of wanting the art to be seen and to get attention. When we put the pieces on the wall, no one judges," she says. In some ways, Barbara always has a hard time considering these collages as "real" art. She attributes that to having studied art history.

"This is more like therapy. Barbara and Audrey are so nurturing, the studio feels very, very comfortable." That's what Barbara C. first noticed when she first came to the studio. She knew right away she wanted to come back. "It's like eating mash potatoes or chocolate. I find collage very comforting.

"When I worked in ad agencies, I never wanted to work as an art director. I didn't want anybody to tell me that something I'd done creatively had to be changed for a client. That's the thing I recognized in collage class. I don't have to change anything or impress anyone," she says slowly, obviously savoring it.

Barbara coaxes a collage out of her thick, black portfolio, and places it carefully on the table. She smiles slyly, remembering back to her first collage. She describes it as "dark," and says it reflects on a really difficult relationship she was in at the time—with a man who had a penchant for fast motorcycles. "I was with a guy who wasn't good for me. That first collage blew my mind. It was the first collage I made in that class. I was going through hell because of the emotional drama, and it all came out in the collage. That experience showed me how powerful the work was. That to me is the crux. That's probably what art is for me."

> Art is the language
>
> that is the language of the heart.
>
> *Margaret Mead*

For Barbara, art is her expression, a vehicle that takes her where she otherwise wouldn't go. It throws light upon her inner life, gives it voice, and gives it a tangible presence. Sometimes she works in a more controlled, intentional way with color and design, but sometimes the art "blows her away" when a piece suddenly transcends her intentions. "That's when it's sacred—outside yourself—that I just think is magic!" she says, enthusiastically. "You didn't know it was in you. That's why I keep coming back. I can't forget it. There's so much more going on in life than what we're feeling and seeing and hearing. We're accessing a whole other level through collage, and that's the most important level. Going deeper to what's taking you on your path, leading your life. I'm just beginning to pay more attention to that."

Barbara had an innate feeling that she needed to do this work, and took naturally to placing her pieces on the wall to look at them with perspective. "Putting shapes and color together and using an X-acto was natural to me. I find

INTO THE LIGHT

Barbara Crow

We're accessing a whole other level through collage,
and that's the most important level.

collage more accessible than painting—I can leave it out on a table and come back to it."

Barbara comes to collage with no preconceived idea of what she's going to create. She brings nothing to class to begin—no folders, no files full of images. She brings only her X-acto and cutting board and then scans the magazines, plucking images she wants to work with. She continues looking for images until Audrey gives us the signal that it's time to start assembling our compositions.

There is a rich array of images to choose from at the studio. Audrey and Barbara J. have been collecting a wide range of magazine donations for over ten years—art and communication magazines, architecture, photography, interior design, yoga, food and wine, high-end fashion, and lots more. Calendars are another popular resource for large background expanses which help set up compositions. The local bookstore, artists, designers, and others who've heard about the work help to keep a steady stream of fresh pictures coming into the studio.

"I select images by shape, sometimes by color, or sometimes I'm looking for something that's easy to cut!" Barbara says, laughing. "Sometimes I'll go with complex cuts. I choose things that I like, or that are pretty, or because I love the texture, or the way it goes with another piece. The things I choose totally form what I'm going to make. But it's strictly compositional, it's visual."

Considering the complexity of the images brings a new dimension into play when collaging. Lots of intricate cutting can add to the texture of a finished composition, and can also show off the manual skill (and patience!) of the artist. Artists are intuitively looking or waiting for something to grab their eye. But is it an aesthetic or a color? What calls to them? Why would an artist stop to cut out one thing and not another?

"Sometimes because it's funny, or it amuses me," Barbara says, offering one perspective. "Maybe it's unusual or evokes some kind of an emotional response. Like a woman looking away that makes me curious, makes me wonder about her." Barbara says she identifies with the female figures in her collages, but not right away. Instead, Barbara chooses images because they are beautiful, it's her aesthetic.

But it could be an emotional impetus too—a figure with an interesting expression. She chooses images that feel personal to her.

Barbara slips through the pages of her portfolio, then stops to show one of her collages. "This was done in March last year," she says, with quiet composure. "My mother was in a nursing home. I chose this image," she says, pointing out a papier-maché figure.

Her mother's health began to decline rapidly in the home, and then she became quite ill, affecting Barbara deeply. The long cavernous hallway pictured in her collage seems sadly institutional. At first Barbara didn't know what all the collage images pointed to, but soon realized they depicted her and her mother.

"Most of my collages are about my emotional state in the moment. This circle is a way to hold my mother, to keep her safe." She pauses, then reflects, "It's interesting that what compels me is the emotional level. I find this beautiful, the way the light is coming through it. This circle mirrors the second circle. I did this collage one week, then I did a second one the next week. We were having serious concerns about my Mom. I was just holding my heart," she says, pointing to a figure in her collage. "There was lots of sadness. This figure is me," she says, pointing to one of the images. "But this other figure I was struck by, because it had no head," she says, pointing to a second figure.

Barbara's mother died two weeks after she composed the second collage. She recalls looking at it after her mother's death and says she was "totally amazed." She describes an inner sense that "we were losing her." When Barbara looks back on this second image, she describes how it depicts her mother going down the stairway and then leaving. She says the figure at the bottom represents the dance after death. "I've done that in painting, and later I see what it was about. This stuff is very powerful. It gets to your unconscious, before you become conscious of what's going on. These two collages were very powerful.

"Your unconscious isn't known to you. That's what it's about for me, when I'm really working—it gives me insight into me. Who needs therapy when you can do this? If I wasn't an artist…." Her voice trails off as the suggestion lingers.

THE STAIRWAY

Barbara Crow

I was just holding my heart,
there was lots of sadness.

YEARNINGS FOR FLIGHT

Barbara Crow

I've just always wanted to have an Airstream trailer!

the adaptive unconscious

This question of consciousness is one of philosophy's oldest riddles. Since humans first began asking the question "Who am I?" the way the brain gives rise to subjective experience has mostly remained a mystery.

Current research on *nonconscious thinking* defines it as an evolutionary adaptation. Much of this "thinking" happens outside of our conscious awareness, woven into our hardwiring as a way to process the thousands of sensory signals coming at us on a minute-by-minute basis. If we can only process a small amount of this information consciously, where does the rest of it go?

The adaptive theory[10] says that the unconscious mind, which has adapted itself to recognize patterns and groupings of information that may be of use, stores much of it. We can later retrieve it to make evaluations, translate meanings, and set goals, in tandem with our conscious thinking.

Barbara's insights are spot-on in many ways when suggesting how collage practice might serve this function. Through mining her unconscious repository, she gains insights into her own feelings and behaviors. Some of the collage students, only half-joking, refer to collage practice as "the cheapest therapy in town!"

Through her education and practice, Barbara has quite a bit of art experience to share. She says she tends to choose emotional, meaningful, or evocative images. But what's the first thing she does after she makes her selections, where does she go from there? What can she tell us about making a composition?

"Sometimes I'll pick a background first, choosing something large that can hold the other images, something intriguing enough," she says. Then she begins to place other images in the background. She tries to balance one image against another, using symmetry, along with shapes and color. It's something she learned in painting—trying to work the entire expanse, not just one area. She keeps moving around the whole composition.

"I try all the pieces after I've collected several and find some of them just belong together because of shape, color, or subject matter. Usually one image emerges as the central theme, something I want to work around." For Barbara, collage is a visual and compositional practice. She is not usually focused on content. She's not trying to tell a story. "I'm not ever trying to be symbolic. Never. It might come out later, maybe. Internal symbolism and mythology is very personal. I take most things at face value." Barbara resists interpreting the work when people want to read meanings into her choices of imagery, color. or visual themes. "Take this one. I've just always wanted to have a trailer, an Airstream!" she says, pointing to one of her favorite collages. "And I like this woman, it's from classical art. It's just her, juxtaposed to the trailer. Some of this is luminosity. I like seeing light and using light.

"It's almost like I'm not doing it," she says, conveying a sense of suspended belief. "That's the best thing about it. My ego is not involved so much. *I'm not doing it.*" Barbara feels like there is something else that works through her. Her sense of time—or her level of consciousness—sinks into a zone. She loves being "in the zone." It neutralizes her. In all of her art-making, Barbara senses this feeling. "When I'm in this place, the world is okay in every single way. To me, art is my connection—this is it."

Barbara's motivation for making art is to go to this zone, to be in the present. She describes it as transcending the ego, getting out of her own way. She's got a blank canvas, what's going to come through today? "It's what channeling must feel like, I suppose."

If Barbara can go to this place of transcendence and the art is without ego, how does she feel about the product? Is she living only for the process of creation? Is the product itself ancillary?

"There are times when I'm not happy with the art," she admits. "In the end I want it to look nice. I want a product that's interesting enough to claim as my own. That's even more true of collage, because I'm taking other people's images, taking them out of context." Barbara says she has aesthetic standards, that she wants the work to look good. Yet another part of her doesn't care. She doesn't want to worry about the final artwork until she's completed a piece.

Barbara refers to the two collages about her mother and points to the stairway piece: "Aesthetically, this one feels chopped up and not so great. Not one of my

SEEN

Barbara Crow

*The collage came together when I saw how
the branch shadows extended the eye lashes.*

prettier collages—but I like it because it has meaning." These personal meanings do arise at times through the personal symbols. She points to the other piece, and says, "This one is prettier. I like the arch and the colors—this one I like better, visually."

Barbara's antidote to her heavier pieces is to create funny collages. It's her way of being joyful, letting herself go out to play rather than feeling anxious about the outcome. She likes to juxtapose elements—for example, classical art against illustration. Sometimes she goes for color or sometimes its opposite, monotones. Sometimes she'll focus on shapes. She is consciously aware of filling in space and balancing sides. She also believes in saving all her collages, good or bad.

In Barbara's view, the group process is a "container." She feels that making collage in the group studio creates a structure, with Barbara J. and Audrey containing and grounding the group. She says that is very different from collaging alone at home. "There's some kind of cross-pollination going on, a kind of osmosis. At the studio everyone is doing the same thing—connecting and talking.

"Then the group show is a nice way to affirm everything. I think of it as a completion, it holds everyone's process. Part of making art—for anybody—is that you want to show it, and there's not much other opportunity to show art." Barbara really enjoys hearing the others' feedback. It helps her to step back to look at it from a distance. Then she sees new things in her work. It gives her new ideas for new approaches. It inspires her to see the other collages and hear what the artists say about them, too.

"I've started dialoguing more, working with my collages at home since I took Barbara Jacobsen's Journey Book class. That has been amazing! I was surprised, because it came so easily."

The Journey Book[11] workshops conceived by Barbara Jacobsen delve more deeply into the relationship between collage and dialoguing. She started Journey Books as a way to develop the artists' stories more fully. Artists start with a finished collage, then dialogue with the images through journal writing, and then finally, produce haiku as a capsule of their writing. Inspired by Robert Johnson's book *Inner Work*,[12] Barbara J. encourages the artists to explore more deeply using "Active Imagination," which Johnson studied at the Jung Institute. Johnson describes Active

Imagination as "the dialogue you enter into with the different parts of yourself that live in the unconscious—similar to dreaming, except you are awake and conscious."

"I journal every day, so I dialogued really easily," Barbara C. says. "I ask, 'What are you doing in my collage?' Then this part of me would just go off. I allowed myself the freedom to do that. I had no censoring around that. I would just make stuff up. There it would go, back and forth. It would just take me. It was so fun!"

Barbara figures her dialogue comes from another part of the unconscious that surfaces, another piece of it. She could do a collage today, for example, and then do the dialogue six months later. Whatever is speaking to her, whatever is being reflected, is what comes alive in the present.

> We don't see things as they are, we see them as we are.
>
> *Anaïs Nin*

Coming up with the words from these nether regions doesn't seem to present a problem for Barbara, who says she works with her "issues" all the time. She knows that we all have things we're not happy about that come up, things that are bothersome. "You know, dealing with the same archetypal stuff—of dark and light, the good and bad, or the big worries of being a bag lady! I just let it come through the collage.

"I've done lots of writing that way. I was in a writing group where we did that. Natalie Goldberg explains it in her book *Writing Down the Bones*.[13] You keep the pen moving. Sometimes you hit a block and you work around it from a different angle. You go to another element or figure in the collage. I think the images are like Tarot cards,[14] your personal mythology. I look at the world that way. Most of the things that one responds to are a mirror, a hologram of your self. The collages are an easy way to get below the surface. I don't remember any of it being problematic, disturbing, or even difficult."

Barbara's practice appears to be one of change and complexity, one of anomalies and of seeming contradictions. She relaxes into the studio ethos of non-judgment, but has her own standards of aesthetics. She never tries to tell a story or to work with symbols, but acknowledges that the work is most powerful when it acts through her unconscious mind. She doesn't want to change anything to impress anyone, but enjoys hearing the group feedback and on some level, wants others to like her work. Perhaps the best descriptions of the practice simply defy definition. To embrace all of the lessons from collage practice may mean moving away from an "either/or" view to a "both/and" world. Perhaps our perceptions and knowledge will always remain incomplete, paradoxical. The real value appears in continuing to ask the questions every week—together, in our sacred circle.

STUDIO CLIPS Try making a collage with images that represent a special theme: birthday, wedding, holidays such as Christmas or Hanukkah, vacation, travel, food, celebrations, career, or graduation. These can be color copied and sized, then sent to friends and family as unique and very personal greeting cards.

YOGA FIRE

Barbara Crow

KADDISH FOR AMERICA

Rona Weintraub

*I discovered that collage opened a way
for me to express my grief.*

"When I meet somebody new, I keep talking to them until I find out what we have in common," Rona says. "My life is all about communication." Rona believes that each person has at least one thread that connects them to any other person they might happen to meet. She believes that each and every one of us has something in common—that all we need to do is find out what that is.

The running gag at the collage studio is how Rona synchronistically finds herself in the middle of the action, knows the individuals involved, or attended *the* event. Bring up a movie you've seen lately and Rona knows the screenwriter. Watch a live program on PBS after dinner—there's Rona in the audience. Go to the symphony and there's Rona sitting in the row in front of you. "I'm lucky to know lots of people," she says, laughing. It only made sense that one of her friends knew Barbara Jacobsen and introduced her to collage.

Rona was reluctant to pursue the classes, though. She had never considered collage and had no interest in it. Yet she did have a drive to express herself creatively. She had tried oil painting, pottery, and photography. With each medium, she learned there was hard work involved in mastering tools and technique—a practice that required patience, diligence, and creative energy.

She knew she'd never be good at any of them until she applied herself. So why did she pursue collage?

"I didn't have to draw!" she exclaims, with glee. Art had not been a part of Rona's early life. She never learned to draw and she had never felt artistic in the conventional sense. She thought she might pursue writing as a creative outlet. But one day Rona decided she'd give collage a try. One day, and she was hooked.

Audrey and Barbara showed her how to start. They took her on the usual tour of the studio and showed her the materials—a box of architecture magazines, a box of nature magazines, the food and wine magazines, the scissors, tape, and glue, the tools. She worked quietly on her own, not paying any attention to what others were doing. "Right away, I looked for a background image," Rona recalls. "It made sense to pick a background, a nice big expanse from a calendar. Then an image drew me, a Japanese garden…and I think there was a Buddha in it. Buddhist teachings were already an important part of my life."

That first collage Rona wanted to make started with the peaceful Japanese garden. Then she added all the things that interfere with being peaceful and calm, clipping out images of items that intrude—soda cans, telephones, computers—and simply started taping them onto the background.

"Then Barbara Jacobsen came over. Of course, she was very supportive and said it was wonderful." But then Barbara began to show Rona ways to make her collage more interesting: perhaps if she cut away this piece of the bush, or slipped the phone down behind it. Barbara didn't tell her what to do; she raised questions and possibilities that piqued Rona's imagination, yet left her to arrive at her own insights. Barbara taught her a few techniques, and just like that, Rona's art progressed to a whole new level. She realized there was more to collage than just pasting things on. When she composed the images, arranged them, they looked even better.

"Then we put the collages up on the board," Rona says, pausing to set the scene: "I looked around and thought, 'Oh my God, look at what they're doing!' These were amazing, integrated images. Seamless images. Collage is not just sticking things onto paper—this was very different. Some of Barbara's collages were up. Whoa, it creates an entire mood, takes you to another world…." Again, just like that, Rona's imagination soared to a new level. She was so intrigued.

When she describes her first impression of the studio as "calm, peaceful, and non-judgmental," Rona is reminded of her meditation center. The artists she encountered were friendly and open. "Barbara and Audrey are really magical. I've had a thing all my life—I'm very judgmental, I'm so critical. It's so hard for me to meet my own standards. This was a place that felt so healing," she says, as her eyes well up. Rona realized there could be some breakthroughs here—and not only with art.

Rona has built a long, successful career as a speech and language therapist. Clear, effective verbal communication is very important to her—being sure people get each others' message as it was intended. Collage was the first experience she'd had in which she could express herself without words—something that didn't happen with any other medium she dabbled with—not with pottery, photography or painting. They weren't as directly affecting for Rona. In collage she discovered representational images with implied meaning that she could put together any way she wanted to make a statement.

When she first began collaging, Rona tried to plan the themes and the imagery of her compositions before starting her work. She quickly realized that finding images on demand was impossible. She doesn't plan any more, has no objectives. Images come her way and she moves them around to create a composition. That improvisational imperative and the spontaneity it requires has been freeing, challenging, and satisfying all at once. She feels her speech therapy practice is like that too—a child comes into a session and she has her bag of tools to work with that child, but uses them in spontaneous, creative ways. Over years of practice, her experience guides her.

"At collage, I come in with a blank mind and not many materials. I do save images though. I have taken images out of airline magazines—I'm so bad! I try not to rip pages out of magazines at doctors' offices. I now realize there are infinite numbers of images in the world, so I don't have to do that," she laughs. "I start new each time."

tikkun olam

Community is the first excitement for Rona when she comes to the studio to collage. She loves talking to the other artists and says she would come even if we didn't collage. She loves sharing. When she sits down, she cultivates a blank mind and looks at the newest magazines available in the middle of the table. She describes sometimes being "in a mood." For example, "a geometric mood." In that case, she goes to the architectural magazines looking for lines and shapes, or sometimes a color. But most often she doesn't know what mood will strike her until she starts looking. A shape, a color, or a theme might grab her. She'll see a fashion image and play around with fashion or beauty. She flips through magazines looking for things that excite her.

You suddenly understand something
you've understood all your life, but in a new way.
Doris Lessing

"I'll recognize a theme or a pattern usually in the first thirty minutes. Let's say I'm working on color. As I'm working, I'll recognize a theme, and think 'Oh wow, I didn't know I was saying this.' The issues I care about often manifest in my collages. I'm involved in peace and justice issues, politics and the environment. I think many people connect with my art because I've communicated a meaningful message. My art often reflects the spiritual, political and social causes I care about."

Then Rona's eyes become intently focused. "I knew I would be a speech therapist as early as high school," she says, and explains: "All through my elementary grades, there was a boy in my classes who had a severe stuttering problem. I wanted to help others like that boy, it was a calling." Rona credits her mother as her role model—"an amazing person, a very compassionate woman, she wanted to save the world." She mentions a Jewish principle—*tikkun olam*—that means to heal and repair the world.

Tikkun olam is a guiding principle in Rona's life. In the 16TH century, Kabbalist Isaac Luria taught that God created a Divine Light, and then created ten vessels to hold the light. But the vessels shattered. The great task of humanity, Luria said, is to raise the sparks back to the Divine and restore the broken world. Today, *tikkun olam* connects human responsibility to the obligation to remedy what needs healing in the world. Themes reflecting such social, spiritual, and political issues flow through

MAY YOU BE PEACEFUL

Rona Weintraub

*My art often reflects the spiritual, political
and social causes I care about.*

AUTHORIZED PERSONNEL ONLY

Rona Weintraub

I see the world as an ironic juxtaposition of things.

Rona's collages, but she won't realize what she has created until the collage begins to coalesce as a whole.

Rona often arrives at class bubbling over with community news. She has devoted herself to various causes over the years—many having to do with restoring the natural world. One of those commitments involves lobbying to protect sea life from man-made destruction. Also a passionate birder, Rona can differentiate avian varieties that all look the same to the untrained eye. "Nature heals," she says. Clearly, she has taken this philosophy of repairing the world to heart. How does she incorporate these themes into her collages?

"In the beginning, I used to tear out lots of images. But now I cut out a background and then flip through and see a few images I want. I love working with one magazine." Early on, Audrey and Barbara challenged the class to work with a single magazine. Rona likes the idea of this finite task, to try to make a collage with just one magazine, because it forces her to slow down, and to examine the images more closely.

"Let me show you," she says, pointing out one of her collages. "I made this collage in my first year. The colors keyed me into the images—gold and silver. Some people say the main characteristic of my collage work is juxtaposition. I tend to see the world as ironic juxtapositions of things." For example, Rona might contrast sterility versus opulence, or reverence versus humor—a contrast of opposites. Sometimes her collages simply capture incongruities.

Rona doesn't set out to use juxtaposition as a way to create tension in her art, but sometimes it does just that. She describes how it happened in one such instance. First, she saw a picture of an ornate cathedral, all in gold. Rona had traveled to countries where she saw many people without enough to eat, and saw them struggling up the steps into the churches, which were wealthy by comparison. She imagined breaking the church apart and giving each person a piece! Then, when she saw an image of a cold, silver-gray vault with the sign "Authorized Personnel Only," her mind leapt to the thought of superimposing these bars over the cathedral of gold as a social commentary. One of her early collages, it always generates interest and lively comments.

Early on, Rona put her work up on the whiteboard without interpreting any meaning at all, but she found other artists engaging with the works, responding to what they saw in her collages.

As she continued the practice, Rona began to see more layers of meaning, too. They were unconscious at first, but she found that the collage process brought new ideas forward to her conscious mind. "This is a very deep psychological process, like therapy," she says.

Rona describes experiencing an internal silence as she works without words. For her, collaging is a visual fugue halfway to a dream state, but the images she chooses "are not by accident." As she makes selections, she knows her conscious mind is extracting a theme because the images resonate with her. But in the silence she's making contact with her unconscious, as if in a dream. What arises is a reflection of something going on deeper inside, and Rona never knows what will come up.

She admits she has a fear of the blank canvas, but feels that collage is less threatening than other art forms because we start with thousands of images, then eliminate to get to artistic expression. She feels less anxious creating this way, finding instead that it stimulates her creative juices.

"At the beginning, I wanted to create something fabulous! I wanted it to be the best! But that's all gone," she chuckles. "After all these years, I have hundreds of collages in my house. Some are wonderful, but the majority of them are not. It's okay. That's the way it is. Photographers shoot thousands of images and get five art pieces."

During her first year at the studio, Rona became aware of two things about herself: that she felt competitive and that she wanted praise. What is most important to her now, she says, is to see what others have created for display. She appreciates each person more, along with the struggles they have in their lives. Rona sees the studio community as an art group, a support group, a therapy group, and a political meeting—all rolled into one.

"When new people come in, I'm much less judgmental." Instead, she describes waiting for new artists' work to unfold. It's a different feeling for Rona now that she's collaged over time. She has become less competitive, less judgmental. She finds great joy in others' successes.

"I empathize with the other artists," she says, her eyes welling up again. "This is very special. I'd been reluctant to open up about myself, in the beginning. It's made me more accepting of myself—things that I like and that I don't like—and more forthcoming about things I used to hide. People in class come out with things they've held back, things they've never told anyone, then we wind up laughing about it."

Rona thinks that because we're working with the unconscious, a part of us is engaged in a process similar to a dream state. We're consciously working with visual images, and we're also "down there, in this unconscious realm. This is the one place in my life where those two things meet, and they're happening simultaneously.... It opens people up."

positive patterns

How does Rona feel about displaying her work and talking about her collages? She appreciates that the dialogue is low key, non-critical. People can say what they want. Then others chime in. "The great thing is that you know it won't be a critique." Rona cringes remembering other art classes where "the focus was on criticism, telling the artists where they missed the mark, what's not good." The collage studio is different in that the remarks are more positive. People make a point of saying something encouraging. "That's a wonderful example to set, for all of us in our lives, to look for what's good."

When Rona takes her collages home, she usually props them on the back of her sofa, where she can look at them for a while. Then she puts them away. If she thinks a particular collage is a good piece of art, she stores it in a folder with others she considers show-worthy. Rona sees her pieces in a new way when she observes how people look at them at the art shows. "I don't know anything about color theory. I've never studied that stuff, or composition. But I know if it's good—it's intuitive. Others also give that feedback. They'll say I have a good sense of design or color."

Rona leafs through her portfolio pieces and picks one as an example of ironic juxtaposition, sliding it across the table. "I love the absurd juxtaposition. Little did I know I could portray humor visually! I call this *The Last Supper*." This collage

THE LAST SUPPER

Rona Weintraub

I discovered I could be funny...visually!

features the classic painting by Leonardo da Vinci. Rona collaged sepia-tone images of gamblers from the Old West sitting in front of the table playing cards as Christ and the Apostles looking on. It's a favorite at the art shows.

"And then when 9/11 happened, I discovered that collage opened a way to express my grief. In the Jewish religion, you wear a black ribbon pinned onto your clothes when grieving—and Kaddish, the Jewish prayer for the dead, is recited as part of the mourning ritual. I call this collage *Kaddish for America*." The piece she shows has a screaming eagle imposed over a black and white striped American flag, with smoke and flames in the background. Rona found all the images at the studio the day she made the collage. She felt a sharp need to express her feelings about September 11 in images. With hundreds of magazines to choose from, she was amazed at the synchronicity in finding these pictures just when she needed them.

"It's so weird...you don't know why you're pulled to that particular box of magazines, or those calendars. I had such deep feelings to express that it was a huge energy release. I put my hand out and the magazines were just there. I couldn't believe it! Sometimes it just comes through me."

Making the 9/11 collage was a welcomed catharsis for Rona. It helped her feel some relief when she had been carrying so much pain inside, when talking about it just wasn't enough. Somehow, creating the art provided a way for her to let go of the anxiety and tension of these distressing feelings. "A way of breathing out into images," she explains, exhaling in one long breath.

Rona also describes a new shift in her work—she wants to do more with abstract images. It's hard for her to break out of realism, to let go of recognizable images, but she wants to give it a try. She also began taking Barbara Jacobsen's Journey Book class as a way to make more time for dialoguing with her collages and writing about them.

"I'd been going to surrealistic art exhibits and was inspired to make this collage. Look how much I wrote: *Time is running out. Stuck person bursts from the cave to accept the world! My relationship with time, not making changes, being stuck, getting out of where I am. Wanting to make changes, but feeling like I'm stuck in concrete*," she says, reading from her journal.

Her image portrays a man emerging out of a manhole, holding the heavy metal cover aside. He appears to be struggling, but clearly wants to get out. What does this bring up for Rona? She wants to talk about "being stuck," in all its aspects. She just kept writing and thinking about how she's stuck, about feeling separate, or hiding from her various communities, or about making commitments. She writes about her family of origin, and about her mother. "I want to dialogue more deeply with the collages. That's why I wanted to take this Journey Book class. At first I thought it was too complicated, I didn't want to make the time, didn't want to deal with the pressure."

Rona looks up from her Journey Book, raises her eyebrows suddenly in high, double arches then furrows them just as quickly, as her mind leaps to connect the dots. She wants to dialogue more deeply, to move forward, but feels stuck! She gets the irony, smiles wryly, and then bursts into laughter.

STUDIO CLIPS Try making a surrealistic collage. Cut out a good-sized, evocative image to use as a background: a long hallway, a building with lots of windows, or a provocative interior with a stairway, or a series of rooms. Now look for smaller images that you can position on this background that might be humorous, out of scale, or scary—or juxtapose images that don't normally "belong" together. Stretch the limits. Mix and match your images, moving them around the page until you are satisfied. Remember to cut into windows, slit areas where you can slip images behind doors, inside windows or partially hide them from view as a surprise element.

MAN DEALING WITH HALF TIME

Rona Weintraub

*Time is running out. Stuck person bursts from
the cave to accept the world.*

BUTTERFLY WOMAN

Lea Alboher

This is how I want to feel.
She's up in the air, supported, trusting.

The sweet aroma of cooked onions wafts out the front door to Lea's kitchen where she sets the table for dinner and closes her workshop in the adjacent garage. Lea buzzes back and forth—a study in perpetual motion. She manages to close down business for the day, all while gabbing and explaining, gesturing with her hands, and finishing the half-made salad, wet and shimmering beside the porcelain sink. She rarely takes time to cook, but today she decided she would.

Lea is one of the few commercial artists practicing at the collage studio. Coincidentally, her commercial artwork is making and selling hand-made clocks, with collage faces and regular clock mechanisms that tell the time. They started taking shape in Lea's art more than thirty years ago when she began selling crafted items as a street artist in Israel.

Lea relates her personal history while nibbling salad and sipping vegetable soup. She grew up in Israel, in a small beach town that attracts tourists, and where her father worked in industrial diamonds, the town's main commerce. She entered the army like most young people there and served for two years. After the army, she earned a degree in textile fabrication, then worked in design and manufacturing for a time. "It was depressing," she says. "Factory work. It wasn't creative enough." Still pursuing her dream, Lea decided to go to art school: "I was insecure about my talent, but I started studying."

In her second year at art school, she was scheduled to teach high school classes, but immediately realized teaching was not for her. She tried work in a puppet theater, dabbled in graphic design, and had a lucrative run as an artists' model. She worked as a secretary. None of it stuck, until she started to make paintings on stone. "This crazy American guy used to sell these painted stone pins from the inside of a big jacket. He would open it up (like a flasher) and show his pins for sale," she says, snickering. Lea began to find her own way to create, experimenting and teaching herself by learning different techniques.

Lea started painting decorative pins, too, selling at shows, and touring in Europe. She left Israel at age twenty-nine, and somehow was drawn to San Francisco. "I only remember I had a friend there, and I showed her my painted stones. She looked at me like I had lost my mind, but I supported myself by selling them, by being a street vendor."

The decorative pins led Lea to create painted ceramics. She began by molding and firing the ceramic, then painting it. She gradually started making squares, then bigger squares until inspiration struck—Lea came up with the idea to apply collages onto the tiles to make clocks. "At that point I started selling only to galleries," Lea recalls. "But the gallery buyers' market was tough and there weren't enough avenues. I was working at home alone and felt isolated. I never had contact with consumers. I also experienced a disappointing, terrible show—and at the same time my landlord raised my rent. Suddenly, I couldn't afford to stay in San Francisco."

Yet Lea remembers that difficult time as a stepping stone to move to Sonoma. "How does a girl from Israel choose Sonoma? The first two years were hard." Lea felt isolated and out of her element in a tight-knit, rural farming community. At least in the city, she had the illusion of being connected to the people around her.

Then one day, while making copies of her collages at a local shop, Lea met some women who saw her collages and told her about the studio and the classes. But she thought "Why should I do collage there, I'm already doing collage!" She could never work with people around her; she felt she had to work alone. "But I believe in the number three—three people told me about the collage studio. When I finally went to class, I sat next to Barbara. I didn't talk much at the beginning, it was overwhelming."

COLLAGE CLOCKS

Lea Alboher

*Inspiration struck—Lea came up with the idea
to apply her collages onto tiles to make clocks.*

a healing journey

Lea had been making her commercial collage clocks for a decade when she started to work with personal collage in her home studio. She didn't think much of her first one, which she created in a therapy session. In fact, she thought it was terrible. She didn't throw it out though, and that collage became the first in her new odyssey of personal discovery.

"I always thought I would go back to what I thought was my real artwork—the photography and sculptures I had worked on for many years," she says. But Lea began to go to the collage classes at the studio and when she started developing her personal collage she thought, "Maybe *this* is my real artwork." When she first went to the class, it opened her eyes to new possibilities. She saw her collages in a new context—that it's not so easy to make good compositions. She gained a new respect for her work and realized she had found her medium at last.

"Sometimes I'm disappointed that my personal collages don't sell. But because I don't sell them, I can go wild with them. I have all the freedom to create whatever comes to mind because I don't need to be dependent on style, color, or any considerations for market—this is the gift of not selling artwork. When you sell the work, you start to sell a part of yourself, without even noticing. When I'm doing my commercial work with the clocks, I have to go with certain colors that will sell, to consider where the hole on the clock face will go…just show me the money!" she wails, only half-joking.

At the studio, most of us who create collages are amazed at Lea's productivity. She usually makes more collages than anyone else, sometimes as many as five or six in one class. She's totally focused because this time at the studio is precious to her. It's her personal time for creative expression.

"I heal myself with my personal art. I journey to connect to my psyche and my dreams. I always get something back, but I need quiet to see what is inside. Everyone has their own way. For me art is important, if I go too long without it I get depressed. It's food."

The biggest benefit to practicing art is "working on our emotions," Lea explains. Art is one of Lea's tools to work on hers. Many times when people feel anger, frustration, or even happiness, they may not have a way to express it. "Artists, do,"

Lea says. "It's healing because we can go to the art and work on our feelings. It's not that I know exactly what issues I'm working on—it's unconscious, like dreams, which help to heal you. In dreams, your psyche takes you wherever you need to go, and your creativity takes you wherever you need, too. It's not a process you can put into words, yet somehow it always takes you to the right places intuitively—it's all on the emotional level."

According to Lea, that doesn't mean the process of healing always feels good. Sometimes it's painful. Yet, she feels one can look back in hindsight to see what good came of it. "When I had immersed myself in fine art photography, it was hell, it was hard," she says. "But many, many years later, I could see how it helped me to deal with a dark time. Through art, you can deal with your stuff, like anger. Then one day, gradually, you start to think, I'm less angry!"

When Lea collages at the studio, she sometimes brings images to class, but she prefers to select new ones. "Old images lose energy, new energy is important," she explains. She has no agenda when she begins to collage, but feels she needs to follow whatever catches her eye. At one time, Lea experimented with using forest images, looking for the ideal forest to collage.

"I suppose it's like the fairy tale *Hansel and Gretel*," she says of her forest images. "But without the scary part—no witch, just a pleasant forest. For example, when I do guided imagery, I think of a place where I am relaxed, I go to some place that makes me feel safe and happy—I would imagine a forest."

For a time, Lea's collages were full of forests and trees. They seemed mysterious, almost mystical, peopled with many different characters with some peeking out from behind tree trunks and others floating in the air. She included various animals and magical creatures woven in among the branches. The enormous range of folklore, myth, and superstition about trees and forests provides an especially evocative theme. Fairies, witches, spirits, and nymphs have come to life through the legends and lore about these mythical places.

Lea slides her portfolio across the coffee table and opens it to show one of her forest collages. "This one I love…*Butterfly Woman*. This is how I want to feel. She's up in the air, supported, trusting. It describes a feeling. I'm totally into using

Artists are healed by their art.

Mary Renault

black and white, with a little color. And lately, I'm into creating a new childhood for myself—fixing my old childhood. It just showed up from my creative experience. I cannot force any of this. Sometimes it just helps to connect with your inner kid."

When she was a child, Lea "cut things out all the time." She always cut papers and images and put things together. Now when she collages, she says she goes back to this place, her source. More than simply childhood spontaneity, Lea believes the child embodies the self who exists before constriction, before adult concerns "cover it up." For years, Lea refused to connect with her childhood. It took her many years to get there. Her father had suffered with debilitating, long-term illness that stressed Lea's family to the brink. Lea's early memories are tied up with the pain and responsibilities of caring for her father, even as a teenager.

Now, art is the vehicle that takes her to this time and space to work on unresolved emotional issues—issues she might not want to face. This "inner kid" can be vulnerable or needy, but by engaging her, Lea feels she can revisit her childhood again and again, with fewer obstacles, fewer closed gates. She can face difficult feelings from her past, finding new healing and freedom each time she does.

Lea also describes how collage practice heals, "like discovering new realizations from a potent dream." And, like dreams, she believes that each collage comes from her unconscious. She *needs* to create, to get to the next collage, in order to make her journey. "We followed a process at class for a while, called *Soul Collage*,[15] from Seena Frost's book," she recalls. "I thought, 'Soul collages? I'm doing it all the time!' From beginning to end, all of them are soul collages.

"Take this collage called *Reflection*," she says, pointing to a richly-hued piece. "I made that one because the woman is relaxed. I'm never that way! But when I saw it, I realized part of me is serene and quiet. That's why I put it up as a reminder.

92

REFLECTION

Lea Alboher

I made that one because the woman is relaxed.
I'm never that way! That's why I put it up as a reminder.

In some collages I see peacefulness. I know it comes from me, but it may be small and needs to grow."

Lea suggests that the collage process mirrors Gestalt work, opening up a whole new part of her. "In Gestalt, you are ten thousand different parts—all you, no one part more important than another. I look at collages that way. They are another part of me, coming to life."

Lea's practice is highly intuitive. She feels if she gets out of the way, her best art happens through a kind of "channeling," which other artists describe too. Lea has a sense of getting her ego out of the way, opening her body, and allowing the work to come through her. She knows she can't force it, but by letting go and stepping aside, she allows the work to unfold. Sometimes she has a great idea and tries to make it happen, but says that it never works that way. "My head is good for business, but not for art. My best pieces come from my stomach, my gut."

Lea considers herself a perfectionist, and since collage is her profession, she *wants* more critique in class. Sometimes she wants to voice constructive criticism of others' work as well, because at times a composition may not work, and she feels there can be improvement. She believes that as students get better at the practice, they can handle criticism. Lea would welcome a more critical dimension to the dialoguing herself, but respects the special quality of the studio and leaves her inner critic outside.

Each student knows they can improve their work by inviting the group to give honest feedback on collages. Displaying our work on the whiteboard is the time for these remarks. Critical comments are not banned. There is no explicit rule on this, just that we should be mindful of how we word our comments.

Sometimes an artist hits an obstacle or block in composing a piece from their selected images. It can be frustrating at times. Constructive comments offered by the group are meant to enliven each individual's vision, to ask evocative questions, and to encourage each artist to raise the level of their work. Usually, most of us forget to ask the group for an open critique.

Each person has an individual vision and different methods to work with, regardless of their training. What informs the work and what motivates each artist adds to the studio experience. We learn from each person in the group. Certain artists raise the bar on the quality from week to week. We are all in awe of the scope of what's possible, at how far this medium can be stretched. Lea is one of our standard bearers. She demands much from herself to induce authenticity through her art and challenges all of us—not only with her finished pieces—but also in her focus, concentration, and her work ethic.

"I highly recommend people to do collage. It's great because you don't have to know how to draw. It's healing. If you just let it happen, let it be, you'll be amazed at what comes up."

A log burns apart and clunks down on the grate in the fireplace, riveting her attention. Settling into the living room after dinner in front of a cozy fire, but immersed in conversation, she has forgotten all about it. Despite the interruption, Lea continues her comments on collage and her healing process.

"Even if I'm not there, the studio is there. So many people are putting so much energy into it. It's a community place. I'm not usually a class person. I can't take classes, because I get too nervous. But over time I've learned to connect with different people. When I started collaging at the studio, I became more open." Even when she can't come to Monday classes, Lea knows the studio is there for her. "A rich, wonderful, multidimensional place that comforts me because I can go there."

the boon

Lea begins to tell her personal journey through her collages, illustrating her points about aesthetics and storytelling through the images. She made it clear one day while collaging, that she is immune to compliments about her finished pieces unless she feels they resonate with her spirit on a deep level. Only then does she feel satisfied with her work.

"I really like this one," she says, flipping over the pages of her portfolio. "This one is very peaceful for me because it looks like a healing. I like my head to be touched; it comforts me.

"Here's another one I made of a man I dated. It made me realize that he was depressed! I discovered that through the collage.

TRAVELING

Lea Alboher

It reminded me there is adventure to this journey.

"This one I did three years ago, before I went to Florida for one of my clock shows. I was freaking out, and had a lot of anxiety." Lea looked at this collage before her trip, and thought about the woman in the image, "She's going on a journey." In Florida there are turtles on the beach, so she staged the collage in her travel van, and it reminded her there would be adventure to her journey. It helped her tremendously. "Sometimes the collages jump, if I can just get out of the way."

Lea continues showing several of her portfolios, leafing through them hurriedly. "Here's one I did when I was so tired. I can't explain it, but there's something nice about being tired. I like how something healing is beautiful. I adore beauty. I never thought of it as a high quality, but now I love it. I love this collage. I think I'm going to put it up on the wall.

"This is me and my mother. She's disapproving." Lea lets a small burst of air out through her nostrils and flips the page. Most of her memories of her mother recall disapproval.

"This is when I started my new collages of children—to recreate a new childhood for myself. This is one I did of my upbringing. My mother always told me she never had nice dresses, so she wanted to dress me well. So dresses and love are mixed up for me."

Then Lea shows a few examples of what we call treasure maps. Usually around the first of a new year, Barbara and Audrey dedicate a special class to make collages to include pictures of things we want to bring into our lives. Lea works on her own to picture things she wants to manifest in her life.

"I went to a workshop on the energies of families and ancestors, and did this one. This is me and my father," she says, pointing out another collage.

Lea's discourse on her journey through art is amazing. The staccato tour through her collage portfolios is full of enthusiastic discovery and insight, yet tinged with the world-weary understanding that comes from years of living an examined life.

"When I was a kid I liked to cut stuff. I would put them in notebooks, cut and glue. No one cared, so I just kept it to myself." Lea always wanted to create art, she was "always rubbing up against it," she just didn't get any support from her family, or signs of encouragement from those around her.

EVENING BLOSSOM

Lea Alboher

"If the collage studio wasn't here, it would be sad, it would affect me deeply," she says wistfully. "Even though I can't go there all the time, it's a sense of community I never had—it's that way for many of us. We've lost it because the extended family is gone; we're getting so isolated. Loneliness is a sickness of many people...."

STUDIO CLIPS Make a treasure map. Select images that represent things, people, feelings, or experiences you would like to invite into your life. These could include things you need, items you plan to buy, a person who represents a love relationship, or one who represents a collegial relationship, or a friendship. You can also look for images that invoke a certain mood, or quality of life to which you aspire. You may find images which represent new qualities you wish to embody, or which represent new ways to act. Compose these images on a larger background, and stage it in your home where you can look at it, and remind yourself of these treasures.

REACHING

Sue Ann Fazio Zderic

I felt connected to all life,
all consciousness.

Deer scatter in all directions, startled by a car winding over the oak-studded hills near Sue Ann's home—a refurbished barn. After months of rain, delicate, mossy crowns on the treetops turn the little bowl where her home nestles into an enchanted, emerald land. Though the rain begins to subside, the sky still threatens with dense cumulous clouds, amplifying the colors all around. Sue Ann appears smiling at the top of the stairs in welcome. The sound of a motor amid the serenity instantly calls attention to any visitor.

"I grew up with a strong spiritual background and sensibility," Sue Ann explains, right from the start. Steam curls from her tea as she gingerly cups it to her lips, checking the temperature. Her eyes—an unexpected blue—hold a steady gaze from above the cup as she continues. "My mother was a devout Catholic, but she was also psychic. And although I was raised Catholic, she introduced me to many other options. She opened doors for me and set me on a deep exploration that has helped me all my life."

Growing up, Sue Ann witnessed a stream of people coming to her mother for clairvoyant readings. Her mother did readings for Sue Ann, too, during her teen years. Her mother didn't "predict" the future or give warnings. Instead, she encouraged Sue Ann to look within for answers, guided her with sage advice.

She gave Sue Ann guidance and support to be herself, and to see beyond material possessions. Observing her mother's psychic readings for others opened up the world for Sue Ann to view things differently. "I didn't see people as only people," she says. "It helped me develop more compassion. My mother would see something in someone's aura (multilevel human energy field), sense and then know more dimensions of that person, unseen dimensions that would affect how she interacted with that person. She taught that there's so much more than meets the eye, and to respect that. That was a higher value than what someone looked like, or how much money they made."

Sue Ann describes how her mother inspired her to discover her own spiritual path, and also introduced her to valuable teachers. Through this circle, Sue Ann connected with a publisher in the Pacific Northwest to work on transcribing the spiritual teachings of a well-known channeler (someone who acts as a voice for a spirit entity to communicate with the physical world). She packed up and left her native New York, moving to Orcas Island at age twenty-three.

"Living on an island, you have to learn to do lots of different things. My creativity bubbled up, mostly in the way I lived my life—creating beautiful gardens, growing flowers. I lived alone for a long time and I collected things. As a child I collected rocks and cobalt blue bottles. I've always gathered and collected found objects. I have a sense for that."

Sue Ann jumps up from her armchair to find a photo album of crafted pieces she made during her time on the island. She displays a heart sculpture made from various colors of beach glass she collected. "Ideas came to me. I've always been interested in folksy, crafty things."

Sue Ann made birdbaths, too, on the island. She created them out of poured cement with local beach rocks and sand for mosaic inlays, selling them through galleries. She made picture frames and mirror frames the same way. She made baskets out of blackberry brambles because they surrounded her home on the island. She just followed her heart—all out of her love for creating. "It's a fulfillment for my soul, an opportunity to take creative energy and think about it, play with it, all while surrounded by artistic people, by patterns in nature—the light, the water. I learned my lessons from nature, mesmerized by light coming in through the windows and landing on salsa bowls at a restaurant where I worked."

When Sue Ann moved to Sonoma, she discovered the collage studio through a chance meeting with a woman at the library. "We were talking about mosaic or collage, and she told me about the studio. A couple of years went by, and I finally called about the classes. I'm so mad I didn't show up sooner!"

It was very easy for Sue Ann to come into the studio and begin creating. "I felt so…embraced," she says, her voice breaking. "It brings up emotion, because I felt such an acceptance and warmth. I felt seen, on a soul level. I needed it, like watering a very thirsty plant. I felt like a kid in a candy store, to have all those magazines supplied, to enjoy the ease of people interacting. Whenever there's a heart connection, I feel like I can fit in."

Sue Ann had experienced collage before—but only fifteen-minute spurts of making quick collages. She had practiced juxtaposing color and various materials in many years of creating mosaics and crafts, but she wanted structure. She wanted to learn more about cutting and technical skills. Like all the other new artists at the studio, she got "the tour," and heard there were no rules. At the beginning she thought she needed to have a plan and used to be nervous about it. It wasn't until later in her practice that she let go of that.

Sue Ann also felt shy about sharing her feelings and how she sees the world. Like so many of us, she's afraid of being judged. "I sometimes get nervous and have a reaction when speaking in front of people. It's embarrassing, it makes me feel vulnerable. I've gotten over that, it's more spontaneous now."

Over time, Sue Ann began to trust herself more and felt that newfound ease carry over into her life, every day. She feels more comfortable as a result of becoming freer with her creativity. "It's a great way to approach each day—a great lesson for life."

Introduced to various spiritual teachings by her mother, Sue Ann also had a strong sensibility to follow her own inner guidance to find her path. She just knew there was more to life that she wanted to experience. Part of her journey led her to practice different meditation techniques.

Meditation practice helps Sue Ann accept the constant changes that unnerve her or threaten to throw her off balance. "Getting out of bed I say the Serenity Prayer," she says, reciting the well-known lines. "It's time to face the world. It's the way I've trained myself to think through my years of meditation—starting with Transcendental Meditation (TM), and then Vipassana insight meditation—to calm my mind. I tend to be nervous. Meditation helps me."

the greatest gift

Sue Ann remembers sitting cross-legged in a room with her TM teacher, receiving her mantra, when suddenly she experienced a powerful shift in her consciousness. "I felt an energy and an opening in my chakras (energy vortices; in Indian thought, centers of spiritual power in the human body), in my whole being. I don't remember all the details now, but I had an altered consciousness experience. It was a physical high, a total change in energy. I felt connected to all of life and all consciousness."

Sue Ann had a second, more powerful awakening a year later. In a hands-on circle where participants are touched in various places on the body by the facilitator, she experienced an opening in her seventh chakra (associated with the crown of the head)—which opened her to an experience of feeling completely at one with the universe—that was the most profound of her life. Again, and deeper still, she felt total harmony and a sense of connection to all life. She experienced an epiphany in that moment: that everything, including herself, was a part of God—that God is in all things. The intensity of it overwhelmed her so much that she cried for days and had a terrible headache!

"Everything since then has sprung from these experiences. This opening has been the greatest gift of my life. My mother supported me on this path, a blessed person who taught me that there were different names to call this power, this source of life—and that we are all part of it." From her mother, Sue Ann learned empathy and compassion. "We all have our flow. The way our lives wind, twist, and turn may be tragic or wonderful, but we are all connected."

Sue Ann feels more at peace to have this understanding—even in this crazy world—that the material stuff is all play, an illusion, that we humans are so much

BLESSINGS

Sue Ann Fazio Zderic

Meditation helps me to accept
the constant, ever-changing life.

THE ELEVENTH HOUR

Sue Ann Fazio Zderic

*My mother was a blessed person who taught me
there were different names to call this power, this source of life.*

more than what meets the eye. Collage helps her to express these other dimensions. That's where her creativity comes in. It's not important for her to talk about it, as long as she has an outlet, an expression through her art. Then she feels the world is not so lonely. "That's art, that's collage, that's nature, and interactions with people in a loving way. That's my connection."

Sue Ann also uses her collage work to express unconscious yearnings. Collage allows the deep, still waters inside her to have a place in the outer world. It allows her the opportunity to look and see these other dimensions of consciousness. With collage, she doesn't know what's going to come out, doesn't know what's going to come up from the unconscious realm.

"By letting myself be still, like in meditation—at first all this crap comes up," Sue Ann admits. "The monkey mind. In order to get to that calm place, it might take a while. Working at the collage studio is so much more potent than collaging alone. There's a collective energy that I feed off, generated by all those wonderfully creative artists."

Creating in the group gives Sue Ann the support of a healing environment, a sacred space that holds each artist. "It's like stepping into a calm place with a candle lit. Or like going to the ocean, or out in nature on a mountain—suddenly you hear the waves, the birds. You hear things more deeply; a power, an energy starts to build. In the studio, all the objects have energy. The art and hangings on the wall, the magazines, they all remind you that you are in the home of creativity."

Earthly things must be known to be loved;

Divine things must be loved to be known.

Blaise Pascal

peeling layers

Sue Ann starts digging through a big, translucent storage bin full of collages to show her work and to talk about her creative process. Sometimes she creates collages with others in mind, like when she makes a card or a gift for a friend. But she wants to allow herself to express from a deeper, more personal place. It's been such a difficult process for her that she describes it as "peeling layers." She wants to take more risks, but feels something holding her back. "When I see the collages others do—they seem fearless!" she says, referring to other artists' experiments, their leaps into unknown territory. "I have no real art training. I don't know technique, so I need to learn by practicing."

Apart from practicing technique, she wants to let loose, to let go of her self-consciousness. Sue Ann wants to take risks or to adopt a broader view of how her collages might evolve. "It's almost cliché, the things I'm drawn to now," she says, wearily, "Water, landscapes, colors, animals, or maybe dancers." Sometimes she collages with Buddhas and things of a spiritual nature. She figures when she's ready to start doing something else, she'll choose different images that stretch her personal boundaries and her art.

Sue Ann describes how her mind reviews and poses questions during her drive to the studio. Her voice takes on a singsong lilt as she lists examples: "How do I approach this? Should I be planning? Should I be thinking about my feelings? What do I feel, what do I need? I'd be driving to collage class, thinking 'Where am I at… what, inside me, needs to be expressed today?'

"Sometimes I have to talk myself into the fact that I deserve this time. I often feel like I don't have enough time. I have to tell myself it's okay to be going to collage. This is for you. Sometimes it's a combination of feeling selfish, or that I should be doing other things—or that I need time alone. It's very recently that I've gotten more at ease, not feeling nervous.

"But there's something special about going to collage class. I ask different questions of myself. When I go to work as an ophthalmic assistant, it's about service. I'm giving. When I go to collage it's about me. It's about turning in to what my soul needs to express. I'm going to see people I feel comfortable with, people

OASIS

Sue Ann Fazio Zderic

Sue Ann had a strong sensibility
to follow her own inner guidance
to find her path.

I like, people that uplift and inspire me. I'll feel that warm acceptance and love, especially with Barbara and Audrey. There is such consistency there. I'm a fledgling artist, who feels insecure. I don't know what I'm going to create. A while back I told myself—make a bad collage! Or sometimes I think I'd like to make a birthday card. Then, I change, and think 'Don't worry about others, just let it come out, allow it.' Sometimes I think 'Don't make a collage today, just clip images.' But of course I'll make something. How many times do you hear, 'I've got nothing done?' Then at the last minute, I'll put images together that evoke something."

Sue Ann's concern is not to get overall approval. She is disappointed that she's not expressing more authentically or more freely. She feels that there may be pretense—or too much simplification in her art. Sometimes she fears she's not tapping into something deeper, not hearing the deeper currents because they're obscured by a blind spot. She feels vexed by her inability to summon—on demand—the personal epiphanies that are so fulfilling with this work. "That's why I meditate. Sometimes with collage, I'm thinking too much about myself, so I take the opportunity to practice meditation by emptying my mind."

That seems like an oxymoron—intentional unintentionality! Even in meditation, to stop thinking, to drop the story, to try not to get attached to the pictures. Yet we find ourselves wanting to find ever more interesting pictures, the high-end art stuff. Sometimes commercial magazines, filled with repetitive advertising, dull the senses. "I can't look at magazines the same way anymore, I go for the gold!" She looks for more and more unusual things, but she shows stacks of images she wants to get rid of. She wants to purge them.

Sue Ann continues showing more of her collages, holding each one at arm's length to examine. In one image, she questions what's happening on the planet. She's attracted to issues on a social level and wants to dialogue more deeply, to explore the images she chooses. Sue Ann feels she has trouble articulating in words, so she enjoys working with pictures in collage to get beneath the obvious. She listens carefully to the comments and intuitions the others may have about her work when the pieces are displayed on the whiteboard. She makes a point to listen with an open mind and heart, detaching from her artwork so she can be more objective.

BATHING IN THE LIGHT

Sue Ann Fazio Zderic

"It's fascinating to hear what others see in my pieces. I'm interested to see it objectively. I don't know what's going to come out. It's like I'm sharing a piece of myself. I may like what the feelings are, but maybe not the composition. *But what am I saying?* I've learned from others. What they point out shows there may be more to the collages than I first thought. I allow myself to put all the parts together: the feelings, the feedback, while seeing it objectively up on the wall.

"I find this work very humbling," she says softly. "Humbling because the story I tell myself may not be the real deal. This work allows me to reveal things I don't want to admit or show the world. I don't know what percentage is the heart of who Sue Ann truly is, or the fluff of who Sue Ann thinks she is. Oh my God, it's humbling!"

All the artists are practicing the same art form, so we're all equal in that regard. Some in the class are more accomplished with technique, yet the process is the same. Even with less polished composition, the collage dialogue can be illuminating.

"Collage is also good for just getting things out, like free writing. Like the morning pages which Julia Cameron describes in *The Artist's Way*.[16] Getting stuff out on the page, writing through the junk to get down to what's real. As time goes by, I'm hoping for more of what's deep underneath to come out. For me it's about integrating my spiritual life into what I call the real fake world. Maybe we can make it more real?"

The vivid tableaux in every nook in Sue Ann's home are testaments to her relationship to art. Her mosaics, bramble baskets, beach glass, stacked collages, and modest altar in the corner all reflect a profound sense of spirit, which she has discovered through creative expression. Together these still-lifes and artifacts make up a collage of her life—wonderful gifts of communion honoring her commitment to make it real.

STUDIO CLIPS This is a good exercise to jump-start your creativity when you're feeling stymied. Pick a magazine like National Geographic, or another magazine containing long articles on a single topic with great photos. Select a story that you find especially appealing, and cut out as many images as you'd like to assemble. The subject matter, color and texture of the paper will all coordinate well. When you're unfocused, or need direction, this is a great way to just jump in.

MASKS

Kate Dumont

Sometimes it's scary,
even after years of doing this work.

"I loved making art in high school and got good comments," Kate says. "But then I forgot all about it because I decided I wanted to *be somebody*, wanted to *be important*," she continues drolly, exaggerating a belief she shed long ago.

After graduating high school, Kate went to live in Sweden as an exchange student. She mastered a couple of languages and found she really liked Europe, feeling more at home there than in her native New York. Once back in the States, she ventured into journalism, veered into political science and considered a career in diplomacy. Eventually, she landed in California.

"After school, I got into solar energy and computer programs, which led me to high-tech." Kate explains. "I liked so many things, but I prefer dabbling, not specializing. All my life I've had great training through my work, learning on the job. Now I'm mostly a tech writer. I learned programming to understand basic electronics, but I consider myself a linguist, not a mathematician."

Kate got work in the San Francisco Bay Area where she began exploring, and discovered Salute to the Arts—an arts and crafts show in Sonoma—on one of her outings. "At that show, I bumped into two very friendly people—Audrey and Barbara!" she says, smiling with the memory. "They were so entertaining, so much fun showing off their collage work. The art had a surrealistic quality to it. I couldn't believe it was cut and paste. It was to the level of fine art. I found it so intriguing."

At the time, Kate was still working on a career in technology, but she began to acknowledge that she really loved art. Eventually, frustrated with corporate life, she quit her job because her health had declined. She suffered with stress. When she saw Audrey and Barbara's artwork at the show, it made her happy. Having studied photography and experimented in the darkroom, Kate thought their collage pieces "looked like photography, but with a twist." In 1996, she decided to take the collage classes for the first time.

"My house has been taken over by collages ever since," she says, laughing. "I have old suitcases full of collages, they're piled up against the wall, they're stashed behind framed pieces, they're hanging on the walls, they've taken over the kitchen nook—they're everywhere! For me, the studio is a community around collage that I find very supportive. When I displayed with the Collage Collective, I learned how to frame an art piece, step by step." Through the Collective, Kate learned how to order frames, cut mats, and string the wire for hanging. Because everyone shared and learned from each other, she felt a genuine sense of community. She says the members have had their share of conflicts over the years, yet it doesn't matter, the group is self-sustaining. These are people who have something to offer, including the support they give each other.

"Who says art has to be solitary?" Kate asks. "Community is…" she begins, then pauses, "I guess you could say we're *collageonauts*! We're willing to go into inner space! Willing to take that risk. Sometimes it's scary taking the risks, even after years of doing the work, but the artists are all in it together." As a group, they allow each other space to go through their moods, to change and grow. According to Kate's view, community means like-minded people. In this community, "like-minded" doesn't refer to consensus, but rather to a kindred spirit they all share. Lively and curious, they are people who are willing to examine their lives—their hopes and fears, the good and the bad—to look at things anew.

"We engage with each other. Sometimes people have gotten judgmental, so we're not perfect, but we go on. Community extends beyond the art. Art is where it started." When Kate first saw Barbara Jacobsen's collages, she felt they were so magical, mystical, spiritual and deep that she wanted to do collage just like those. But instead, she says her first collages were ugly monsters, both literally and figuratively. Her first art piece pictured a matador standing in front of an armoire, with a huge, ugly moth-like insect emerging out of the dark closet. She thought, "I am not sane, I am not a healthy individual." She made one ugly collage after another! But Barbara and Audrey told her, "Kate that's good, that's scary—you're in your monster phase. Lots of artists go through it. In time it will shift."

Kate had to face her demons. She realizes now they represented her fears. She sees collage as a dialogue with her deepest self—the self that is not so accessible. But Kate didn't want her art to be that way. She wanted it to be something people could enjoy—beautiful pieces; beautiful and powerful. Instead, all her monsters came out. Barbara and Audrey prompted Kate to dialogue: *What are the monsters trying to say?* She finally understood what the monsters' images stood for—and then the guilt, the shame, and their stories emerged. Audrey and Barbara guided her through it. She says she might have stopped, because of her inner resistance to the painful feelings, but persevered because they encouraged her. The dialogue comes in its own time. Then, as the months turned to years, new collages emerged. Different phases came out in Kate's art over the years—different colors, different themes.

"I was not the kind of person who could easily access my emotions, or identify them. The collage gave me a sort of book to read—my Rosetta stone, a key to decipher these feelings." Although some of these early collages upset Kate, she feels now that the hard work produced growth and change that otherwise may have eluded her.

"There are lots of emotions that I don't show, it's personal. In all my art, that's what's happening. For example, I've had very early memories come out in my collages. Take my blue butterflies, for instance. I made all these collages with blue butterflies." Years after making these collages, Kate remembers sitting outside on a summer day at four years old, trying to catch butterflies. But she proved too slow and clumsy, so instead she decided to sit and watch them. She became very still and they landed on her. A blue one landed on her knee, and she became fascinated. It brought her into fantasies of flight. Since then, Kate has always found butterflies and birds magical. "And Barbara and Audrey always go to the metaphor—birds and butterflies are messengers, a communication between heaven and earth." As a writer, Kate wonders how that relates to her: maybe these symbols bring information emerging from her unconscious to inspire growth and change?

BLUE BUTTERFLY GIRL

Kate Dumont

A blue butterfly landed on my knee when I was four.
I was fascinated. It brought me into fantasies of flight.

"Barbara and Audrey also talked about how the collective unconscious might use the butterfly symbol as a metaphor, too," she says. Then Kate started collaging "birdmen," figures that combined male bodies with bird heads. She went for the raptors—owls, eagles, hawks. But she kept thinking, "What is wrong with me?" They were so weird. She felt uncomfortable, felt something wasn't right. Then she worked with them, switching the images around to make bird bodies with male heads, so the birdmen became angels. As she explored, angels appeared in her art more and more. "I don't know if they were rescuing me psychologically, I just don't know."

dialogue with the shadow

Kate's monster phase brings to mind Jung's work with the *shadow*. Jung first used the term "shadow" to describe the unconscious, repressed, undeveloped, or denied parts of the Self. Most of us become divided in the acculturation process to exhibit only socially acceptable traits and behaviors, and to hide the negative, denied parts where they can't be seen. The shadow is that which is not fully allowed into consciousness. We can learn about the whole of ourselves by learning about the shadow and most easily identify our shadows by looking to see what we project onto others.

We will often project the parts of ourselves we have disowned—most likely these are reflections of our own shadows. There, we can see them outside of ourselves. Since the process is unconscious, we tend to think these negative traits belong to others, when they really belong to us. The opposite can also be at work when we project what we admire onto others, or where our talents lay—a sort of golden glow. Ultimately, Kate's collages became her teachers, producing real lasting growth and change.

"I feared that I would go off the deep end, I would go insane if I became an artist," Kate explains, referring to her distress over her birdmen figures. But when Barbara and Audrey told her, "You made angels," she decided she could live with them. And by focusing on this mythical tangent, she could confront her fears every week. When another artist went through a similar period making scary images, Kate told him, "You're just going through your monster phase!" Kate confesses that she actually had serious doubts about her sanity around this time: "I had to work through lots of layers of fear and mistrust.

"In her book *The Artist's Way*, Julia Cameron talks about fears and blocks to our creativity. She calls them creative monsters. We can have creative roadblocks that tell us we can't do art because we'll go insane, or a whole list of things—I'll become an alcoholic, or I'll lose my livelihood, lose my status—a long laundry list. Barbara and Audrey could walk me through those fears. They jollied me along. They would say, 'Wow that's scary, but *good scary*. Are you scared? Wow, everyone's scared—that's a good one.' You could accept your feelings here."

Kate feels that Barbara and Audrey lead by example. She remembers that Barbara made some dark collages at that time too—death imagery. Kate finds it comforting that people can explore any image which represents any emotion, any state of mind. She feels that ignoring difficult emotions is not so healthy, so it's better to talk about those feelings instead. "Now I look back and see the insights I got out of it. The insights I gained were remarkable. It's not what I expected—for me that was powerful. I didn't have any psychological tools to take care of my life. But the images, and the dialogue with the unconscious were powerful. Once the scary stuff moved off, the mystical stuff came out. Something shifted."

Typically, Kate comes to the studio without images or ideas to jump-start her work. In the past she would see something on TV she might want to explore, but when she tried to find images, she came up empty. Instead, she flips through the magazines provided at the studio to find an image she likes, or she looks for a background. She explored black and white for a while, interspersing the black and white with small bits of spot color. "I also went through a blue phase," she says.

"When I went through my blue phase, I cut out blue—a blue sheep on a blue hill, against a blue sky." At one point, Kate just wanted to cut out flowers, but thought it too cliché. Despite that, Barbara and Audrey encouraged her to go with her instinct. She now considers them some of the best collages she's done.

Kate had studied principles of composition in earlier photography classes that prepared her to work with background, foreground, depth of field, and cropping in her collages. She experimented with other aspects of form as they emerged in various ways in her collages from class to class. At first, she created some unusual collage

SENDING LOVE TO THE PAST

Kate Dumont

Collage gave me a sort of book to read—
my Rosetta stone.

OMEN

Kate Dumont

9-10-01 It seemed as if the souls were going up to heaven.

compositions, like her original birdmen—where she positioned the bird heads on poles sticking up from the men's shoulders. Then Barbara made some suggestions: "Maybe you can put the heads right on the shoulders, like a seamless image."

To learn more technique, Kate asked other students about their methods. "But back in those days, I felt cranky. I didn't like it when people approached me, on my collage territory! But then I started looking at art differently. I looked at life differently. I got on what I call my artist eyes." In the beginning, Kate tried looking closely at the collages, to discuss them. She would look very closely, reading the images like Braille. Over time something kicked in, a new way of looking that brought her to a new level of composition, a new way of seeing.

"It also asked of me, what is your unconscious trying to tell you?" Kate describes the collage class she attended on September 10, 2001. That day, for some reason, everyone had created images reminiscent of fires and explosions, which they thought strange at the time. The students put the art on the wall as usual, and discovered this unusual theme running through all the collages. At the next class, after the 9/11 disaster, Audrey asked the students to bring their work from 9/10 so they could look at them. "That day I had cut out white birds, going in all different directions, around this dark image with water and a bridge over a river. I arranged the birds, all flying up. It seemed as if the souls were going up to heaven."

The mystery of the eerie, fiery imagery, as well as the soulful doves, emerging in class the day before the attack on the World Trade Center's twin towers remains precisely that: a mystery that defies explanation. No one suggests this group of artists had a collective premonition. At the same time this enigma is fascinating to consider for those open to such reflection. However, the element of mystery is always present in collage work, beginning as it does with a simple act of selecting colors and imagery from a vast array, and then in the theme and composition that emerges as the artist works.

"There is lots going on under the surface of life," Kate says. "If one doesn't express it, eventually it comes out anyway. The spirit wants to be heard. Any of the arts can express that—interior design, gardening, raising a child. For me this is so fun. If Jean Paul Sartre said 'Life has no meaning,' why not make up our own meanings? Jung said we recognize individual symbols and collective images.[17]

If you go back into different cultures, the angel image is all pervasive. That's what collage does, it helps us to explore new avenues, and create new meaning."

In the 1980's Kate went to an art workshop in Los Angeles, where facilitator and conceptual artist John Baldassari presented "boxes of stuff." The artists found all kinds of things in those boxes: kitchen items, yard tools, knick-knacks—just about anything. Baldassari dumped the items on a big table, then asked each student, individually, to sort them out. Not one person sorted the same way—one would sort by shape, another by color, yet another by size. Kate feels it shows how the creative mind works—how each person makes different, very personal connections and associations, which is just the point Baldassari wanted to make.

Everything has been figured out except how to live.

Jean-Paul Sartre

Sometimes Audrey or Barbara will challenge students to try using images from only one magazine during a class. Even though we all use identical copies of the same magazine, the collages look nothing alike! In one of these classes, four of us cut out the same image, yet each of us composed it in completely different ways. Collage is a container for memories, for our projections, our compositions, and our visions. It's a holder for all these things.

"I think it's very sophisticated to put pieces on the wall without judging them, but instead, to describe them," Kate says. She feels that the dialogues that we have with the art are the best part of class. We describe the imagery—how it does or doesn't work for us. We can't say it's good or bad, or that we like it or don't like it. Instead, we learn to be specific about the elements. The feedback is typically informative. We sometimes move images that are taped (not glued) around, as a group, and learn from this method, too.

"I don't know half the time what I'm putting up on the wall," Kate says. "When the other artists describe my art, I think about what they say. These artists are intelligent,

UNTITLED

Kate Dumont

perceptive, experienced. I usually take it in and think about it." Kate feels that we all bring something to the table, that each of us contributes valuable opinions and points of view. The important thing to do is to learn to listen.

One artist hung her work on the whiteboard—an image of a female figure facing a cold, hostile environment, looking very vulnerable. When tacked on the wall for the show, everybody seized on the overarching element of fear in the collage. After discussing this ominous feeling, one artist observed the female figure more deeply, saying, "I think she's brave." That comment caused all of us to look at the collage in a whole new way. Although stress and fear seemed to dominate the image, the flip side is courage. It was a profound moment. "Just to stay alive is brave!" Kate exclaims. "Facing life and death is what it's about. It's what this work is about."

As we practice active listening and not judging, being open to experience, and engaging together, these practices tend to overflow into other parts of our lives. "In my work, I have to present visual material," Kate says. "Now I can design on a page where text and images can find a balance. The collage classes have helped me professionally. It's given me a better design sense, greater color sensitivity. It's made my creativity stronger. That's exciting. In little ways, life is so much better."

Collage practice has enriched many other areas in her life as well. She has learned not to take things so personally. Barbara and Audrey told her, "When you show your work, you'll hear lots of comments. Remember it's the art they're talking about." That subtle shift of insight has carried over into Kate's relationships in the outer world, too. She realized that if she became defensive about others' opinions, then the dialogue with them would end. If she felt closed inside, she'd be closed in relationship.

Because of the ethos of the class, we are careful and specific as we describe the work, rather than judge it good or bad. It's a style that parallels a method of nonviolent communication[18] that some of the artists have studied and now practice. It's a method that's clear, compassionate, and respectful. It keeps the dialogue open. "I can see when I'm getting defensive, then I can unplug, and can step back. I can allow the comments, hear them, then to ask questions to go to the next level of exchange." As a result, Kate says, "I have more poise and grace and balance in my life now."

More than anything, Kate wishes the studio could be open more often. She craves being there. It's a touchstone for her, a meditation: "If God is a creative being and being creative is being like God, it's my longing to be closer to the Divine. It's also wonderful being around the other artists. I could create in solitude, but I like the collaborative setting. When I'm at work, I have some social outlets, but it's not the same. The people are not as open, not like the *collageonauts*—they're a breath of fresh air!"

STUDIO CLIPS Find a few magazines with diverse images—both full color and black and white. First, select a black and white background image of any size, which can hold several more images. Now select several, smaller, color images to compose onto your background. You can layer, cut, juxtapose, or randomly fit images together any way you like. The outcome will be a black and white image with "spot" color that catches the eye, or surprises the viewer.

Childhood Redux

Kirk Hinshaw

*Part of doing this work is a way for me to show part of my personality
that you don't see, unless you get to know me.*

Warrens of look-alike trailers crowd together on both sides of the narrow street. The mazelike corridor, jumbled with planters, corrugated carports, and cul-de-sacs holds little room to turn around. Soon, number sixteen floats into view at the end of the drive.

The screen door squeaks and yawns on its aluminum frame and the afternoon sun floods Kirk's trailer through random windows, throwing pools of light across the woodwork. His converted trailer, set up with high tables and flat storage, sometimes doubles as living quarters, and every nook is used to maximize the space.

Kirk raises his six-foot-three-inch stature out of a vintage wheel chair. "I used this chair for years when I worked in advertising in San Francisco—it glides so easily on carpet," he explains, his soft Southern drawl peeking out beneath his gentle manner. Although he never used the chair for any injury, Kirk suffered a serious accident after he left his job at the agency. "I fell off a ladder onto a concrete pad while trimming wisteria and broke my hip. I was lying there on the concrete, terrified, looking at my right foot splayed out in an unnatural position. Then my survival mechanism kicked in and I found myself thinking, 'Something good will come of this.' It was a matter of stopping, slowing down, taking a deep breath. That's what finally got me going to the collage classes. It was a matter of finding the time."

Kirk worked in advertising for thirty years and knows that to talk about one's work, to show one's creative work in an open environment is a vulnerable thing. Yet, people walk into the collage studio for the first time and are made to feel safe enough, and supported enough to do something they've never done before. Audrey and Barbara have helped so many people on their various journeys through the collage work, and their journeys take all kinds of roads.

Kirk grew up in rural North Carolina in the 1940's. He says his life was "saved" by teachers and a principal at his high school who took an interest in him and nurtured his abilities. He received recognition for art in grade school when asked to do projects like painting posters and bulletin boards for holidays. His most vivid memory of art was drawing a horse in the fourth grade. "Fellow students made a fuss," he says, "and the teacher came to my desk." That recognition and support made all the difference in the world.

There was little emphasis on education in his home as Kirk was growing up. His mother had run away from home when she was a young girl, with only a sixth grade education. She raised her son, mostly on her own. Kirk's earliest years were spent in a farm community where he and his mother tended pigs. In school Kirk resisted straight academics, but found himself staying up all night creating art to go with required reports, intuitively following his heart.

"Luckily, I had two schoolmates my senior year who found a professional art school in Richmond, Virginia and they brought me a catalog," Kirk recalls. He applied and was accepted, attending for four years taking painting, sculpting, drawing and liberal arts, in addition to the advertising art curriculum, with enough academics to get a Bachelor of Fine Arts degree.

The Vietnam War raged as Kirk graduated from art school and he thought he'd be drafted like most available young men. At the same time, he was plucked from his graduating class for a job at a leading design and photographic firm in Detroit. It turned out to be one of the luckiest things that ever happened to him. Because he went north to the design firm, Kirk had his military physical in Detroit. With a history of back problems caused by a car accident at seventeen, he went through the military physical twice. Luckily, he was put on reserve, but probably wouldn't be drafted. "If I'd taken my physical where I was raised, with fewer people to pick from, sure-as-hell, I would've gone to war."

Instead, Kirk stayed on and worked for several design and advertising firms for four years, at first assisting photographers as a gofer setting up backgrounds, lights, and carrying equipment. He had the chance to shoot his own work, too. He had studied photography and could use the studio and equipment in his off time. Kirk worked eighty hours a week, at two dollars an hour. "That's how old I am!" he exclaims.

Kirk says these first jobs in photography and graphic design studios felt like "paid graduate school." When he advanced in his career to art director in advertising, his art education and professional experience gave him an edge. Yet surprisingly, even though Kirk had earned a BFA and worked in design firms and advertising agencies for thirty years, he never took time to develop his own art.

"I pretty much turned my back on art after art school," Kirk says, somewhat sheepishly. "I thought it was too exclusive. Some of the students at school could be smug and arrogant, even condescending." Abstract art was big at the time and it brought out an intellectual elitism that he felt was exclusive—an exclusion of people because they didn't understand it. He realized only later that part of his outlook was rooted in his own vulnerability. Here was a kid from a rural, unsophisticated background suddenly in school with people who were more cultured. "In retrospect I'm very sorry. I wish I'd pursued my own art sooner," Kirk says now.

revisioning the past

When Kirk first saw one of the collage shows in Sonoma, he was swept away by the surrealism. He liked the disparate imagery put together in ways our eyes and brains don't normally see. Like in a Magritte painting, a bird can fill up a whole room. These surrealistic collages excited Kirk enough to go back to his art practice. He pulls a portfolio from the nearest file, opening it to the first collage he'd made in class.

"People are always amazed at how seamless my images are," he says. They sometimes rub their fingers along his collages, because they can't see the cut marks. They can't figure out how he does it. "I used an X-acto knife in graphic design for thirty years, if I didn't get good at it, shame on me!"

Kirk attended the collage classes on Mondays for about three years pretty regularly. He was usually the only man in class at the old studio then. "I'm more comfortable with women. My stepfather was a Clark Gable type—very handsome, very tall, a strong symbol. But he was a long-distance truck driver and wasn't home much, so my mother raised me or left me with other people to take care of me. There was lots of domestic violence around me in the South when I was young. They didn't beat me, but you can't sort that out at five or six. It can be scary for a child."

Over time, Kirk found himself exploring many facets of his identity through his collage artwork. One of the aspects he examined was growing up as a man in the South and all that goes with that—including the enormous pressure to be "manly."

"When I look back over my collages, I find a revisiting of the childhood I never enjoyed," Kirk says. "My mother, having no other male in her environment, co-opted me to be a life partner." Kirk would go to the post office for her, go to the bank, and sometimes had to go the door to tell debtors they had no money. She had a lot of secrets, too. In retrospect they were silly things, but they tied Kirk to her game of collusion. He had his first job at age twelve in a restaurant, where he worked eight hours a day, six days a week, all summer. His childhood was seldom free of responsibilities, so this collage art began to revitalize his imagination and joy.

Kirk rarely starts his art with a predisposed concept. He just gathers imagery and begins. At the collage studio, he pulled from the magazines he found there, but he admits to being a bit of a pack rat—he also uses images and found objects he's saved through the past forty-five years. There are clowns and masks and some scary images in Kirk's collages, all mixed together. The images are complex and surreal; he combines elements that don't seem to belong together. These diverse elements are scattered throughout his portfolios.

"It stimulates my brain in a way I don't necessarily understand," he says. "To me there's a whimsy." Kirk explains that because of his size—and because he used

RIVER SPIRIT

Kirk Hinshaw

*It stimulates my brain in a way
I don't necessarily understand.*

to have a full beard—people were afraid to go into his office when he worked at the ad agency. He was absolutely stunned. He couldn't imagine why they would be frightened of him.

Collaging became a way for Kirk to open up, to show more of his true personality. "I don't know if everyone is struggling with their identity in some way and trying to say, 'Hey, there's a me inside here.' Maybe I never allowed that to be expressed in other ways, that only here with collage it's safe and reasonable and I could allow that to happen." In the class, Kirk found himself getting emotional—he had found a vehicle that allowed him to show people another view of who he was. Sometimes he would be overwhelmed by emotions, would tear up trying to explain himself and his newfound joy in the work.

Through his art, Kirk felt he could begin to express more of himself through whimsy. He admits it had been "locked up." In the beginning his collages were dark, serious, and very moody. Even in art school, he tended to use dark colors—blacks and grays, purples and blues. When he started to work in class with bright colors, it took him some time to get comfortable with that, but comments about his work were positive and encouraging, despite the discomforting feelings that his surrealism engendered in some of the other artists.

"The journey that was really most powerful for me was beginning to use my own childhood photos in my collages," Kirk says. "I know some psychotherapists are using collage in their work, but I think more should do it." Kirk says collage has been a liberating practice for him, and could be for others. He thinks more of this work could be introduced in therapeutic settings, especially because the materials are so accessible and so inexpensive.

Kirk's early journey through collage was dark and brooding, but the more he worked with his own childhood images, the more he found the brightness and cheerfulness emerging. He could feel a lifting in his heart and soul.

"I practiced at the studio for two-and-a-half, or three years, before I got to these," he says, pulling out another portfolio. His eyes brighten, as if the memories alone contained the power to lift his spirit. He opens the page to a collage with a black and white photo of himself at around age six—the first use of his own image

MOTHER AND DADDY ED GET MARRIED 1947

Kirk Hinshaw

*The writing in the background is from
one of my grade school report cards.*

in one of his collages. Kirk had compiled the collages in this portfolio roughly in chronological order, so they are a valuable visual record of his journey.

"My mother liked exotic things—things not many had in North Carolina," Kirk explains, pointing to elements in the artwork from the Far East. Asian artifacts, balloons, Kachinas, rabbits, cats, masks, and antique toys crowd together in the frames of his collage. "I may have a mind that has a hard time focusing!" Kirk says, laughing. "Do you know how many people are afraid of clowns? I'm a bit of a mask freak, too—clowns could be part of that. This one is my Little Lord Fauntleroy." He points to a picture of himself at age four in a suit with short pants, his hair in an old-style bob, looking very much the little prince.

Lightness came into Kirk's life when he started using his own childhood pictures in his art. The collage that is the most powerful for him is the one in which he was able to cobble together a story, where he began to understand a piece of his identity in a new way, beginning with his relationship with his mother.

Negative memories of her many regrets and complaints haunted Kirk around the time of his mother's death. She felt abandoned by her father, who refused to talk to her for five years because she had divorced her husband. She felt people were always talking about her. She always cast herself as the victim of their gossip, and in a way, pulled Kirk into this "victim" scenario.

Then, just before his mother died, Kirk read some letters she'd written. He retrieved a box belonging to his stepfather out of storage, as she had asked him to do, cutting the rusty lock to open it. Pulling the letters from the box, his attention was riveted by the dates on the letters—dates that revealed a lie. Kirk suddenly realized that his mother had taken up with another man while she was still married to his father.

"No wonder her own father wouldn't talk to her!" Kirk exclaims. "Her father was a deacon in the Methodist church, her husband had gone off to fight the Germans for the freedom of America, and she ran off with a married man who eventually became my stepfather! I must admit I was quite upset, even after she died. We were so incredibly close for so long—but at the moment, it felt devastating to learn that the most important relationship in my life was built on a lie. I felt co-opted."

Kirk felt the sting of betrayal again when his mother died. She left instructions that she didn't want a service. He felt certain she had arranged it so people wouldn't talk about her affair—she would literally take it to her grave. Meanwhile, Kirk had been looking at a picture of the two of them—him and his mother—lying there on his collage table for months. "I went through this bizarre thing where I was reluctant to use this picture of my mother and me in a collage because I thought it might be the end," he admits. "I thought it could be the end of my art, completely. There was something going on, and once that's done...."

Kirk felt that if he found a resolution, there would be no more grist for his art—but what happened turned out to be a special gift. Kirk began to see his mother, not only as a mother, but as a human being. He realized then, that she had done the best she could, she had tried to the best of her ability. "My mom was desperate to make a living, had no education...what the hell was she supposed to do?" he says, straightening his posture. When he finally came to see her as a person, these insights cleansed him of his anger and resentment.

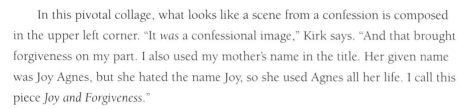

Everything in life that we really accept undergoes a change.

Katherine Mansfield

In this pivotal collage, what looks like a scene from a confession is composed in the upper left corner. "It *was* a confessional image," Kirk says. "And that brought forgiveness on my part. I also used my mother's name in the title. Her given name was Joy Agnes, but she hated the name Joy, so she used Agnes all her life. I call this piece *Joy and Forgiveness.*"

Then he points out more of the elements in his collage. "Here's a Russian egg. With Russian eggs, each one reveals another tucked inside, like secrets. Then, here are the dice—the roll of the dice, meaning chance. And here's a salamander, the mythical creature that lives in fire. The red cloak conceals a male figure. If you look

JOY AND FORGIVENESS

Kirk Hinshaw

This one is the most interesting for me
because the story was so clear.

at the shoes underneath the cloak, they're men's shoes. He looks into darkness, where you can't see. Most amazing of all, to me—none of these images surrounding the portrait of me and my mother were selected consciously."

into gold

Kirk acknowledges how powerful changes emerged through his work on this collage. Through mining his personal symbology, and uncovering these feelings regarding his mother, Kirk gained valuable insights which changed his point of view. He found a tool to separate himself from his mother's myth and discovered a genuine sense of freedom, a sense of himself liberated from a mired past. Before he could truly see his mother as a separate, unique individual, Kirk says the collage relieved his feelings of having been betrayed.

The collage work at the studio also gave him the energy and a springboard to pursue his own mixed media artwork. He still collages on his own because it brings back the lightness when he gets too serious. Working on collage also launches his momentum when he gets stuck. After he stopped collaging at the studio on Mondays, Barbara and Audrey asked him to come back to present a one-day workshop about using family photos.

When all is understood, all is forgiven.

Ernest Hemingway

"I felt confident that I could do the family photo workshop because of the strong experience I had," Kirk says. "I was insecure about it, maybe a little self-conscious—Barbara and Audrey do such an amazing job with their classes. But with the family thing, I thought I knew what I was talking about." Kirk got unnerved halfway through his workshop though, as the artists became very quiet, intently focused on their work. He was impressed by the collages they composed.

One artist had a very tumultuous family and an especially difficult relationship with her sister. As an antidote, she chose to collage an idyllic English garden with a serene look, in order to revise her past and perhaps generate new energy for the future.

Another woman in the workshop had borne a child later in life, after her own father had died. She created a collage of her father and her son, and behind them included a photo of herself as a young girl as a way to bring them all together. "I have a friend, Cheryl, in San Francisco who has been asking me to come down to do a workshop on collage using family photos, too," Kirk says.

The collage experience has helped so many people on their various journeys, often opening up new territory to explore. Kirk's experiments with collage have brought him a unique and powerful tool to reclaim his childhood. By examining his own story and patiently exploring his past, he has found new ways to express the different facets of his identity.

STUDIO CLIPS Collect a small group of family photos, including pictures of yourself. Be sure to make copies, which you can cut and use, especially if you don't want to ruin the originals. Clip around individual images, discarding backgrounds or extraneous items you will throw away. Select a background image of any size from a magazine, calendar or catalog, with ample room to hold your family "cut-outs." Now, select and add any number of additional images to compose onto your background, along with your family photos. You can cut, layer, juxtapose, or randomly fit images together any way you like.

ILLUSIONS

Kirk Hinshaw

I still collage on my own because it brings back
the lightness when I get too serious.

A QUESTION OF FAITH

Cecilia Hong

This is my all-time favorite, even though it's only three pieces.
I love the little boy—he's a cutie-pie.

Becoming Transparent

The odd clutter of outdoor furniture strewn around the entrance to the art studios looks like preparation for a garage sale—or maybe a party. On a steamy Saturday in June, the collage studio is open for drop-ins, but the oppressive afternoon heat has driven almost everyone outside. Cecilia stands next to the collage table, pointing to a three-dimensional piece, talking earnestly with another artist who nods and murmurs in soothing tones that meld with the dense air. Barbara Jacobsen sits nearby on a stool, fanning herself with a magazine, listening with rapt attention. Cecilia's three-dimensional collage stars in the unfolding story, an assemblage that she produced in one of Barbara's Journey Book workshops.

Cecilia first heard about the collage classes when she received a collage as a gift from a client in her busy acupuncture practice. "Just looking at it was so intriguing," she says, "I had to find out about the classes. It's not like I can draw or anything, but I can tear paper! I thought I'd just show up and find out what was going on. Plus, I was new to Sonoma, and I thought it might be a nice way to meet people in the community."

Cecilia recalls her first class as "kind of bizarre." There was no order, there were no rules. She thought she heard Audrey give the instruction not to cut out any squares, so for the whole class she made sure to cut out circles and curves, but no squares. She thought it was odd, but somehow it stuck in her mind, so that's how she approached her first collage. In the end she realized it actually made a more interesting composition! She and Audrey laughed about that later when Cecilia told her about the misconstrued instruction.

Cecilia attended the classes regularly for about four years, and also exhibited her collage work in public shows when invited to join the Collage Collective. She became good friends with many of the people she met through the studio, people she still calls friends today. "We met to show, but also to have fun together," Cecilia says. "It was a gathering of friends to share work everyone was doing, to have community. Collage was the link."

stepping out

At first Cecilia was intimidated by the thought of making collages. "Lots of people at the class were really into art, some had art backgrounds. They had been doing it for a long time. I was intimidated by putting works together and putting them up on the board at the end, but I decided I would." As usual, Barbara asked the group to talk about their pieces and how their collages came to be. That was something Cecilia had never done, so she was reluctant at first, but the group was so supportive and so nurturing, that she just "stepped out there."

Sometimes Cecilia chose not to display her work, or she would leave class early. She noticed she was usually the first to finish her collage. When she was done, she was done. She figured out she could just leave, so sometimes she just gave herself permission to do that. Usually everyone works for the whole time allotted. "This was my social time, so I just gave myself permission to leave," she explains. "The way I did collage was to come in and look at the pictures. I would go into some kind of inner space, then I was done. I always finished a collage, but I never worked on them when I got home. I never put them up. I never thought about them. Sometimes I would just leave them at the studio…

"When you look at your life, there's constant progress and change from when you are born till when you die. That's what the collages are for me, a record of my internal process. I know how others like to sit and look at their collages—often gleaning new insight—but that process doesn't seem to work for me. If I let the collages go, throw them away, then it seems like my journey can progress. There's more fluidity, a flowing. When I keep them, it's stifling for me. I'm creating boundaries. And my whole thing now is to be expansive."

Cecilia says she uses collage as a kind of therapy, as "an internal releasing." At first, she felt she didn't have any real grasp, any deep understanding of the work, so she let the process unfold until she could find an expression for it. Until that happened, she just kept collaging. Results came as things inside her "loosened up."

"What I'm really looking for is a change in my perception and behavior. I don't have to label my feelings, I don't need to verbalize. I may look at things and say, 'Oh, that's sad.' But when I'm in an intense period of making lots of collages, there's a shift that happens. There's a different response in me, in my reactions to the world."

In moments of quietude, Cecilia perceives that her feelings have changed. For instance, using anger as an example, she sees that situations no longer irritate her the way they once did. Confronted with the emotional triggers that used to set her off—a frustrating moment or someone's thoughtless comment—she no longer jumps to anger, is no longer annoyed by these same irritants.

"Collage allowed me to do that, and the community helped me to do that." Cecilia feels it's easy to become isolated living in a city, to never really have any personal contact. But when one is part of a small community where everyone knows each other, there are connections that can be made. Once the connection is made, people can start to blossom.

"I feel like I was a one-dimensional person, and I needed to become three dimensional," she says. "And becoming three-dimensional also means becoming transparent—allowing all the different aspects of who I am to come forth and have a voice, to have an expression. Collage was the key to unlock who I was, to become a full a human being. Before that, I could define myself by my interests, and what I did, merely a biography. There was no heart connection, I was not fully present. I think I was hiding. I didn't know how to break out, how to integrate into this world. Collage revealed that. There were aspects of myself, I had no idea were there! Both the positive and the negative. Once I discovered that, I had to be more authentic. Everything that I was to become, everything I believe in, required that I be a full human being, not just one-dimensional."

Focusing on doing work on this personal level in her acupuncture practice at the same time as she practiced collage, Cecilia recalls an ongoing internal dialogue. Collage was a different way of expressing that, another layer of it. "The group was a new experience for me. I am a very solitary person. When I came to Sonoma, that was no longer an option for me, so I had to find out what community was, how to be in community and be comfortable with it, and to honor my solitary nature. This was a perfect place to engage that." Since Cecilia identified more as a loner, it seemed possible that living in a small town could bring her out of her shell.

"I had to engage on a very intimate level in my acupuncture practice, too. In order to do that I had to be vulnerable." She felt she couldn't distance herself by thinking 'I'm the practitioner, you're the client.' She knew that if she wanted to practice holistic medicine, she'd have to engage with the whole person. She believes it's an equal exchange. If the client doesn't feel Cecilia is as engaged and as open as they are, there's something missing in the interaction. Cecilia creates an equal relationship of direct, open interdependence—very much like Martin Buber's philosophy on dialogue.

"We all have a closet full of masks," she says. "And depending on where we're going, we bring these little masks out. If I'm going to a social function, I bring this mask out. If I'm meeting my family, there is another mask. If I'm meeting my clients, I put on my professional mask." But Cecilia discovered she doesn't want to waste her energy that way. Why not be transparent, open in all her relationships? She figures it's best to be her authentic self. Cecilia realized the more transparent she could become, the more freedom she would have. That's the payoff for transparency—freedom.

"Ever I am, is what I am—it's not good, it's not bad. Instead, it's making the effort to go beyond your own judgments. If you go beyond them, it doesn't matter how others see you. It's all perception. Eventually, the only person who will judge you is yourself—so drop that, too. My passion is health and healing, I think about it every waking moment. What can I bring to my practice to help my clients? That's where all my energy goes."

The collage experience was a springboard for Cecilia's entry into the community, filling this process of inner dialoguing, and doing her inner work. Part of the reason she collaged was for her own self-healing. "The whole thing led me to heal myself, to find my authentic self." That was her major thrust at the beginning; to discover, finally, what her wants and needs were. Until then, she had created an image of what she *should have been*. Now Cecilia had to find out who she really was underneath—the essence of what makes each of us unique, defines each of our quests for meaning.

"That question started the whole unraveling, the whole continuing dialogue. First, to find out who I was. Second, to heal parts of myself that were wounded. Three, to find out what I wanted in life, what life meant to me." Then she began to question even that. Cecilia felt she should question *everything*. "So that's my dialogue all the time, in my head. It just keeps up! Sometimes I tell myself when I go to bed, that I will not dialogue, I will not dream, I will just rest!"

A lot of synthesis occurred for Cecilia in Sonoma. She feels it's the perfect place for her to do this internal work, for her own personal reasons. Collage was the best way to express what was inside, until she could work through her feelings. Language felt clumsy, and working through imagery came naturally and flowed more freely.

gifts from the ancestors

Now Cecilia turns her attention to the three-dimensional collage she described earlier—photographs of what looked like family members, especially photos of her mother. "At first I didn't use any images, but practiced writing haiku for Barbara Jacobsen's Journey Book class," she says. "Then I remembered Caroline Myss saying on one of her audiotapes[19] that you need to acknowledge and look at the gifts you've received from your parents. I could have gone my whole life with this adversarial relationship with my mother, but when I heard Myss say, 'Look for the gifts,' that stopped me in my tracks. Just stopped me! I had been repeating an empty mantra, saying 'I appreciate all that my mother did for me,' but there was no feeling behind it. I had to find that, to find the feeling behind it."

Cecilia's assemblage released feelings of appreciation, and she experienced a strong visceral response. She sensed new feelings of freedom in her body, she

ASSEMBLAGE

Cecilia Hong

Cecilia had begun collecting images, when finally she sat down
one night with her TV tray and took out a piece of foam core and
started cutting it without thinking.

no longer felt contracted. "Lots of us have had adversarial relationships with our parents, whether it's part of one's growth or maturation process or what. I knew that to look at the gifts, I'd have to get through the resentment and resolve some of those feelings I had with my Mom. It didn't involve talking to her to get through it. It wasn't her process, it was strictly my process."

Cecilia joined the Journey Book workshop with Barbara to extend her writing around her relationship with her mother, and to produce a finished book of her journey. She wrote poems, but didn't start collating them, or creating the book. "I didn't know how to make a book, I hadn't been doing anything! A big, fat zero," she says, shaking her head. Instead, Cecilia simply began collecting images and thinking about how to proceed, when finally she sat down one night with her TV tray and took out a piece of foam core. She started cutting it without thinking, without caring what would happen. Then she went to the internet and took clipart images of waterfalls, volcanoes, tropical flowers, and butterflies that looked like the environment where she grew up in Hawaii.

She had pictures of her mother and included other family members too. Under the dim light of a fluorescent bulb, she began writing down her haiku. She only worked at night, cutting out circles. She cut them and pasted them together as three-dimensional flowers, stopping only to allow the glue to set.

"I was determined to make something because I was too embarrassed not to have a finished product to show," Cecilia admits. "Interestingly enough, I found haiku was the best way to express myself, just thinking in short snips. Intuitive associations. If someone asks me direct questions, my initial reaction is to freeze, because that's always been my initial reaction to my mother. Whatever I did wrong, like cutting school, I would get lectured and I would sit there, blank. So if someone

WEAVING-LEAF

Cecilia Hong

I learned this weaving technique
from another artist.

prompts me, then I get out of that mode of being frozen. It took me a while to realize that was my pattern."

Cecilia begins to display the few collages she saved over her years of collaging. "I learned this weaving technique from another artist," she explains, leafing through her portfolio. The collage she points out employs an intricate, painstaking technique. Cecilia used two separate magazine pages, each with color images, and cut them into half-inch strips with an X-acto knife, being careful to leave the strips intact on one side by not slicing all the way through. The result was a vertical page of paper strips and a horizontal page of paper strips, which she then wove together. One page serves as the warp, running lengthwise. The second page is woven in horizontally, as the weft. It looks very complicated and time-consuming.

"Not really. It's a study in texture, colors. I only look at form and color, not symbols or content when I'm creating. And this one is my all-time favorite, although there are only three pieces to it," she says, pointing to another collage. The collage pictures a small child with gold coins looming against the provocative background of multiple Buddhas. "I love the little boy, I love his face; he is a cutie-pie. I was thinking about form a lot, material form. Even within the Tibetan Buddhist tradition there's this emphasis on form. We've lost the essence of experience by focusing on form. You've got to build a stupa, you've got to tithe money." The very paradoxical nature of Taoism always seems to lead us back to what underlies "The Way" of earth, of nature, and even Heaven itself—the ineffable. "So I go back to the Taoist tradition, if you can name it, or see it, it's not the true Tao."

Cecilia continues leafing through her portfolio showing her less serious side, an ironic and playful sense of humor. "I thought this was a hoot," she says, showing a quirky piece with an owl whose head is turned upside down, a telephone dial, and a lopsided clock face, making interesting suggestions. "Silly humans!" she mimics.

"I also like snakes. I created a huge piece—three yards wide, all with snakes. Then I decided to try to do a small one. I wanted to make a piece that was a balanced and pleasing composition using all these images.

WHAT A HOOT

Cecilia Hong

Silly humans!

"This collage is one of the several weaving pictures. I had to cover a word from the magazine page. The interesting thing about weaving is to keep the integral part of an image while weaving another image into it. Sometimes they're successful, sometimes they're not. I'm really focusing on composition. I'm amazed when people can tell a whole story about their collages!"

Cecilia says the collage studio has been a significant part of her growth, of her unfolding, for which she'll always be grateful. "Maybe I'm wrong, but I think Sonoma is unique. There are lots of special people here. And thanks to Barbara and Audrey, and their commitment to the studio."

Cecilia carefully packs up her belongings and collages, then meanders back down the hallway to the parking lot. The scattered furniture has been artfully arranged and party guests arrive just as the wilting heat begins to soften. The guy behind the makeshift Tiki bar offers her a drink as she passes by, then toasts her anyway when she declines and heads for home.

SNAKES

Cecilia Hong

*I wanted to make a piece that was a balanced
and pleasing composition, using all these pieces.*

STUDIO CLIPS Find two, large, colorful images (or abstracts) of about the same size in a magazine or calendar. Cut the first one into vertical, half-inch strips with a knife, being careful to leave the strips intact on either the top or bottom, by not slicing all the way through. Cut the second one into horizontal, half-inch strips with your knife, being careful to leave the strips intact on one side. The result will be a vertical page of paper strips and a horizontal page of paper strips. One page serves as the warp, running lengthwise. The second page is woven in horizontally, as the weft. Try weaving them in a way that retains an integral part of one image, while weaving the second image into it. The result may surprise you.

CELEBRATE

Phyllis Finney

It makes me very happy to be here!

Creative Community

Throughout these chapters, we've heard stories from artists that point to collage as a metaphor for significant aspects of personal discovery, as well as a psychologically- and spiritually-engaged life. We've seen how collaging invites us to uncover the ways in which the tools, techniques, images, and kinesthetic involvement so naturally correspond to the various dimensions in relationships, inner journeys, personal growth, and spiritual connection.

Audrey von Hawley and Barbara Jacobsen dreamed of a place where they could explore avenues of self-expression with others who were similarly driven. Collage became the vehicle, the mechanism to explore these personal insights and render them to the collective. "I tried for years, by myself," Audrey says. "I rented a studio, I showed up and sketched, but I still didn't know what it was about. I didn't know how to jump-start myself."

"I think we're group animals, really," Barbara says. "We're fascinated with each other. It's human nature to want to be part of the tribe. Audrey sent out an email, a Hopi story, saying we are now in the Eleventh hour. The river is rushing fast, people are scared, they want to hold onto the bank. But the story says, let go—go right out into the middle of that current, into the river and see who's there with you. Who is your community?"

How we tap into "flow" moves us into the deeper currents where we encounter ourselves, where the collage artists experience a communal way to animate their life stories through the power of art, and to share those stories with each other. "It's key to see how important the story is," Barbara says. "To see how strong the ancient pull is to storytelling, to the oral tradition. We've lost a lot! There was a time when people had to remember the myths to tell them."

Symbolizing our own self-stories through collage holds the possibility of finding new understanding in frozen constructs we may have held since childhood—or may lead us to new engagements we've only dreamed of. Once we dig deep into the source of our own myths and beliefs, we can own them and move toward a more current ideal, transmuting them into what is true for us now. The collage process is a ritualistic way of approaching those parts of ourselves that may be outside our current window of awareness—either disowned parts of ourselves, the "shadow" that Jung talked about, or some new awareness that is gestating in our active imaginations and about to blossom.

It's best not to over-intellectualize the process but instead, trust it to do its work. However we approach it or nurture it, the collage artists are engaging in an unpredictable, but fertile field of possibility. And although the discoveries seem to emerge out of unknown depths, by the time they are fully-formed they may bring new light—or at the very least, creative satisfaction—to the artist who surrenders to the game.

Even as science and technology illuminate the complexities of the human mind, there are mysteries worth exploring right under our own noses. A compelling statement in an essay by Saul Bellow[20] quotes Terry Teachout: "We are not accustomed to thinking of art forms as technologies, but that is what they are." The craft, skill, technical knowledge, and mechanics of collage are all technologies through which we engage our various journeys. Ultimately, the meaning behind the material world is contacted—not through the physical senses—but through deep intuition. Connecting intuitively with the personal symbols in our imagery is a key to the riddle. In a wonderful metaphor for transformation, new things are made from the many pieces of our lives as art nourishes and renews us.

A PEACEFUL JOURNEY

Justine Filipello

I like to express myself around people...

the art of living

When we think of community from previous generations, we might think of people banding together for survival—building things, sharing resources, or dividing up communal chores to keep body and soul together. What is it that makes up community in our time? How many communities are there? Why do art in a group?

Justine, at twenty-six, the youngest member of our tribe, lives alone. She explains what it's like for her to find community. "I like the noise and I like being around people. Even when I just hear conversations, hear people laughing, having fun, I can feel the energy, the happiness. Just to be around the energy is very cool. I like to express myself around people, and have them express themselves around me."

Working in a group can help accelerate one's art practice, too. "There's no way I could develop my eye working alone," Carine says. "Seeing the whole process of collage—how it develops—helped me so I could begin to pick out images. I didn't get it at first. I didn't know what to choose. I was pulling blanks. It's the practice together, week after week, going and seeing. A picture is truly worth a thousand words. It's the image that does it.

"Community is a group of people that has common purpose, common philosophies. I think about my neighborhood with events like holiday parties, or coffee with a neighbor. It's comforting." Carine says community means getting together regularly, where you see people grow and change. She also observes that raising kids connects one to a larger community. "I raised kids, but I'm out of that now and I've also retired from my job. I've come in and out of different communities. There are different phases in life, you begin again."

Because collage is such an elastic medium, it can contain everyone's dreams, anyone's vision. Whatever can be conjured from the mind's eye can find its way into the world through collage. It serves as an all-inclusive container, or maybe a better word might be *portal*, through which our dreams and visions emerge. We find community as we see each other grow and change.

"I saw a quote the other day that said, 'Home is not a place you live, it's a place where they understand you,'" Robin says, talking about the group work. "I cross the

IS ANYBODY THERE?

Carine Rosenblatt

I've come in and out of different communities.
There are different phases in life—you begin again.

LEAVING MY FATHER'S HOUSE

Robin Chantler

True community is where I feel supported and nurtured,
and where I give that to others.

threshold to the studio and I can be who I am. Every time the door opens, another heart walks in." Robin loves the conversation; sometimes she's chatty, sometimes she's quiet. She learns about books, movies, recipes, and travel, where to stay in Spain, and how to download onto a laptop. She likes being in the circle. She experiences it as joyful and authentic. "Everyone is the real deal in their own way, yet very different from each other."

"The collage studio is a group without a formal agenda, so there's no need to reach consensus," Janie says. "We're not trying to agree on anything!" Janie is a marriage and family therapist who integrates an eclectic blend of traditional and alternative modalities in her work. "Even though I've been a therapist for years, I'm surprised how deep this collage work is. It's exciting to see issues I've dealt with in therapy manifest through art."

"There are no real rules," Robin adds. "It's always changing. We get a suggestion, for example, to work only in black and white. There are no *shoulds*. They don't should on you! The thing that makes the studio work is that it's non-competitive. Everyone is good, everyone is right, everyone is true. It's all collaboration." Robin says that her favorite part of working in our circle is getting to know people through their work at a deep level. We might work at the studio with the same artists for months, and never hear details about their lives, but we get to know each other at a deeper level—that deep knowing that develops when people put their work out there. It's not just about art.

The combined effect of the experience is greater than any one individual or the sum of the parts. The potency of the group synergy is like a final collage: when combined, the images make up a greater whole. There's an interesting alchemy at work that includes all the parts, yet transcends them. We've all experienced groups where the energy was not integrated, where there were gaps in communication, or people vying for control. What makes the difference between synergy and disaster? How can we ensure that we follow a path that leads to a successful group dynamic?

evolving spirals

Usually artists consider themselves independent and non-conforming. As free-thinkers, they tend to break all the rules. Artists also tend to use unlikely means to solve challenges and to creatively combine elements in ways that may not be obvious.

While many groups may begin by establishing rules and hierarchies, Audrey and Barbara began from a different perspective, based on their vision of group work: they accepted what each artist brought to the table. When we value and respect these more subjective qualities and trust the deeper inclination, we gain new insights and risk new levels of experimentation. We begin to learn through collective experience and through making the right combinations. The artists contribute to the mix while retaining their individuality. This is no small matter, but the rewards are worth it.

The lasting revolution comes

from deep changes in ourselves.

Anaïs Nin

Throughout this book, we've heard stories from artists who gained self-knowledge and described personal epiphanies in the process of collaging. These discoveries, these qualities, begin to inform their self-image, as well as how they relate to others inside and outside of the studio. This is one of the biggest ongoing benefits of group work, which may not be measurable at first, may not even be evident. Sometimes these subtle shifts are only realized after a substantial time of integration.

Sue Ann talks of how working in the group has made her less self-conscious, helps her trust herself more in various situations. She credits the group model as one that enables her to move past her hesitation. "I was more self-conscious, thinking about outcome," she says. "Now I'm not. I've learned from watching all of you. It's come over time."

164

EMBRACING HEAVEN AND EARTH

Janie Johannes

The group energy is nurturing, alive, light.

Justine says classes have taught her how to interact with people in new ways. "My friends see me as loud," she admits, chuckling. "But when I'm at collage, I'm the quiet one. Class has taught me a lot by being around older people, because they respect me. I take that and go into other things. When I go into my floral classes, I take in the ways I've learned to be at collage class. I know how to talk now, how to get feedback. It's grounded my personality a lot, just coming to collage. I don't know how. It's just sharing art and being creative, working with color, shape, and form."

The group practice has taught many of us to observe others more deeply, to be better listeners; to know when to make a contribution and when to keep silent. The collective wisdom is a great resource. Listening to other artists enriches almost every area of our lives. We listen to each others' stories, we listen to each artist describe a collage, we listen to the banter that colors our time together— whether we learn odd tips to solve household repairs, or how others resolve personal issues.

New dimensions might open up at any juncture if we're willing to experiment in the studio. Rona says she discovered she could express her sense of humor through collage. She loves expressing irony and absurd juxtaposition in her art. She came to that through practice, by observing what others had to say about her work. She enjoys working that angle and having fun with it.

The group practice has provided a model for Kate, as we practice active listening, not judging, being open to experience, and engaging together. "It's enriched every part of my life, to be honest," she says. "I've learned not to take things so personally. All my relationships have shifted." Cecilia discovered how to plug into the collage group in a very personal way. "I think I used it as a therapy, almost as an internal releasing," she says. "I felt like a one-dimensional person, and I needed to become three-dimensional."

Lea feels that even when she can't come to class, the group studio is her spiritual home: "If it wasn't there, it would be sad, it would affect me. Even though I can't go there all the time, it's very important to me." Barbara C. was clear from the start: "Lots of this studio work is about community…this warm and accepting place. I just felt like I wanted to come back here." Kirk agrees:

WOLF

Audrey von Hawley

The wolf is in the pack,
and the pack is in the wolf.

"For people to walk into the studio for the first time and be made to feel safe enough, and supported enough to do something they've never done before is enormous."

The wisdom of the I Ching reminds us: *The planet is covered with communities, each with histories, traditions, customs, freedoms and limitations. They are communities of towns and cities, communities of career and special interests, religious and philosophical communities, or communities of racial or familial ties. They all run very deeply through time and space, and all share common experiences that bond them intricately within themselves.*

If nothing but the desire to make sense of life, in all its messy, painful, glorious, and surprising moments, Monday collage class—more than art lessons, more than the sum of the parts—helps us expand our hearts, our minds, and our intuition to a higher octave, forming a framework for the creative rhythms below. Through our work with collage, we enhance our creative energy, and nurture the natural unfolding and enfolding cycles of life.

One day, in a deep sleep near dawn, I had a horrifying dream: throngs of snakes were chasing me, attacking me, as I frantically tried to run away, attempting to hide—but they were everywhere, menacing. Then someone in the dream picked up one of the snakes by its tail, and began swinging it around like a lasso, working up speed to throw it at me in one lethal blow. I was petrified. That was all I remembered, then thankfully, I woke. There was no end, no resolution to the dream. I only felt relieved to be awake and out of danger.

Later that same week, I took a walk on a quiet back road in my hometown. Sauntering along the gravel shoulder, I looked down and spotted a perfectly flattened, yet perfectly preserved snake, about fourteen inches long. It was completely intact, tail and head, and had ended its life with its jaws open, revealing a delicate mouth. The scales randomly flaked and fell as I picked it up and gently inspected it. It was as dry as a bone, an interesting artifact. I carefully placed it in the trunk of my car, inside an old manila folder so it wouldn't break apart.

A few days later I suddenly realized I could try incorporating my found object, the snake, into a collage. I felt I should try working with this animal symbol, since it seemed to be calling to me through the dream, and now through this specimen. I brought it to class, along with a few other images from my files. I'm not sure how it all happened, but during class that day, two other artists gave me more snake images. I ended up with about six of them. I finished three collages—all with snakes

ANIMAL WISDOM

Lindsay Whiting

This is where the mystery—
and real magic live.

in them—that astonished all of us. I knew from the other artists' reactions that I was working with something powerful. Aesthetics and composition pale in comparison to these archetypal images, which go so much deeper in our psyches.

But that wasn't the end of it. After class, I went for a walk with one of my classmates. We shared a picnic, then meandered back to our cars along the paved path. Suddenly I gasped, grabbing my friend as we came to an abrupt halt. We were face-to-face with a forty-two inch long King snake lying across the footpath! Milky white rings formed a concentric pattern around its chocolate-brown body. We couldn't believe it. Earlier, we had been together in class when I told the story about my dream, then created the collage using the dead snake. Now here was a live King snake coming to punctuate the story. The snake slowly sensed our presence, then slid around and slithered into the brush. We looked at each other laughing, shaking our heads in amazement.

What does all this mean? Why does it matter? The snake had appeared spontaneously in my dream. It appeared to me again, in the guise of road-kill. When I incorporated it into my collage, I decided to engage with it further, to listen to what the snake had to say to me and to invite its wisdom. But when the live snake finally crossed my path, my conscious mind was stunned into silence.

Weeks later, I still hadn't been able to put into words any final lesson from the snake encounters and the imagery that had so fully engaged me. In some ways I didn't want to, afraid that turning the experience into a conscious one could rob it of its real power. And that's the way it has remained. To this day, the facts are vivid: the dream, the roadside relic, the collage, and the picnic encounter with the King snake. The meaning remains unexplained—and that's fine with me. I'm willing to allow the snake's guidance to live through me as I integrate the feelings and senses it aroused in my own animal nature. This is where the mystery—and real magic live.

[1] Angeles Arrien; *The Four-Fold Way; Walking the Paths of the Warrior, Teacher, Healer and Visionary.* HarperSanFrancisco.

[2] Robert A. Johnson; *Inner Work.* HarperOne, New Edition.

[3] Ray Oldenburg; *Celebrating the Third Place: Inspiring Stories About the Great Good Places at the Heart of Our Communities.* Marlowe and Company.

[4] R.L. Wing; *The I Ching Workbook.* Bantam Doubleday Dell, New York, NY.

[5] Eligio Stephen Gallegos; *Animals of the Four Windows; Integrating Thinking, Sensing, Feeling and Imagery.* Moon Bear Press.

[6] C.G. Jung; *Basic Writings of C.G. Jung; translated by R.F.C. Hull and Violet S. de Laszlo*

[7] Wallace Stevens, *The Man with the Blue Guitar.*

[8] C.G. Jung; *A Symbolic Life; Miscellaneous Writings by C.G. Jung;* translated by R.F.C. Hull.

[9] Joseph Campbell; Diane K. Osbon editor; *Reflections on the Art of Living; A Joseph Campbell Companion.* HarperCollins, New York, NY.

[10] Timothy D. Wilson; *Strangers to Ourselves; Discovering the Adaptive Unconscious.* The Belknap Press of Harvard University Press, Cambridge, MA & London, England.

[11] Barbara Jacobsen; *Journey Book Workshops,* Sonoma Collage Studio. Sonoma, California.

[12] Robert Johnson; *Inner Work.* HarperOne, New Edition.

[13] Natalie Goldberg, *Writing Down the Bones; Freeing the Writer Within.* Shambhala.

[14] Mary K. Greer; *Tarot for Your Self: A Workbook for Personal Transformation.* New Page Books; 2ND Workbook Edition.

[15] Seena Frost; *Soul Collage; An Intuitive Collage Process for Individuals and Groups.* Hanford Mead Publishers.

[16] Julia Cameron; *The Artist's Way.* Jeremy P. Tarcher.

[17] C.G. Jung; *Man and His Symbols.* Macmillan.

[18] Marshall Rosenberg; *Non-Violent Communication; A Language of Compassion.* www.cnvc.org.

[19] Caroline Myss; *Energy Anatomy.* Sounds True Audio CD.

[20] Saul Bellow; *Writers on Writing; Collected essays from the New York Times.* Times Books, New York, NY.

I want to thank the following individuals for their generous contributions to the material costs of publishing this book, with my sincere gratitude. Their subscription represents a growing network of artists and community in support of the Sonoma Collage Studio and Paper Lantern.

Aileen Gell

Americon Yankee Electric

Anne Marie and Stephen Massocca

Art Exchange Gallery, San Francisco

Barbara McRae

Barbara Nichols

Beatrice P. Biggs

Bert and Araminta Blackwelder

Bill Smock

Beverly Rose

Bob Berner

Catherine Sevenau

Charles D. Randall

Checks & Balances

Chris Monroe

Christiane Vincent

Claire Demas

Connie Butler

Connie Mygatt

Cynthia Whiting and Paula J. Marshall

Dale Metzger

Dana Dillard

Dana Dubbs

Darnell Rudd Mandelblatt and
    Corlies Rudd Delf

David Hill

Dave and Anne Whiting

Dede and Ken Goddard

Denise Kelly and Chuck Fernandez

Diane Tegtmeier

Dianna Jacobsen and Peter Ray

Donna Paz Kaufman and Mark Kaufman

Dorothy Van Soest

Elena Sheehan

Eliska and Randy Meyers

Elvin and Alycia Case

Eric and Ellen Joss

Eva M. Westberg

Financial Fitness Center:
    Lois Leynse and Anne Lowry

Frances Freewater

Fred Finkelstein

Gail Goldman

George Maurer and Suzanne Pucula Maurer

Georgia Deaver

Hal Zina Bennett

Hope Mineo

Ian and Kari Van Gelder

James Zderic

Jamie Spooner

Jean Ryan and Cindy Beckwith

Jennifer and Scott Fearon

continued

Jim Madden

Jimmy and Lili Layton

Joan Pechanec

Jon Hubbell and Fran Hayward

Jonathan Frieman and Moira Brennan

Joseph Peter Carucci

Joyce L. Johnson

Julie Wilson

Judith Olney

Judy Theo Lehner

Karen Clausen

Karen Lauderback

Kate Geddes

Katherine Hall

Ken and Diane Neyer

Kimball and Jane Allen

Kizelle Aromatics

Laura Anderson

Laura Chenel

Lauren Clausen

Lauri Clausen

Leslie Jaquith

Lila and Neville Rich

Lin Marie deVincent

Linda and Larry Howell

Lisa Kellman

Mary Ann Hurlimann

Malatee Sirapo-Ngam

Maggie Bedord

Margie Sherman

Marilyn Artieres

Marjorie Lewis

Mary Connolly

Mary Johnson Grove

Matthias Jakob von Baeyer

Maureen Lomasney

Melanie Miller

Merikay and Bill Wisely

Michael and Susan Krieger

Michael Stocker

Michael Zimmerman

Michele Helms

Moona O'Toole

Norman and Susan Joss

Paola Gianturco

Pat Biggs

Paulette Engler

Peggy Burks

Pete Perry

P.J. Tyler and Wally Brueske

Remmy and Paul Kingsley

Reuben and Joanna Pickering

Robert Jeffery

Roberta Alexander

Ron Scolastico, Ph.D.

Robert and Diane Hulme

Rosemary Gong

Rusty Cuevas

Salli Rasberry

Sharon Howard Constant

Silvia M. Viera, Ph.D.

Stacie Goodsell

Susan Ito

Sylvia and Bill Crawford

Ted Whiting, Jr.

Tehra Braren

Teresa Carnes Whiting

Thea Greenhalgh

Thelma Kidd

Theodore A. Whiting

Tracy and Scott Allen

Virginia Farr

Zac and Lolly McCormick

Zak Zaikine

FOR MORE INFORMATION ON COLLAGE CLASSES OR WORKSHOPS

email: Lindsay@paperlantern.biz

TO PURCHASE BOOKS OR BROWSE OUR COMPLETE CATALOG

www.paperlantern.biz
or call: 877-935-7750 toll-free